Pearson Scott Foresman

Leveled Reader

Teaching Guide

Glenview, Illinois • Boston, Massachusetts • Chandler, Arizona • Upper Saddle River, New Jersey

ISBN: 13: 978-0-328-48444-7
ISBN: 10: 0-328-48444-X
8-PT-13

Table of Contents

Graphic Organizers

Introduction

Scott Foresman *Reading Street* provides more than 750 leveled readers that help students become better readers and build a lifelong love of reading. The *Reading Street* leveled readers are engaging texts that help students practice critical reading skills and strategies. They also provide opportunities to build vocabulary, understand concepts, and develop reading fluency.

The leveled readers were developed to be age-appropriate and appealing to students at each grade level. The leveled readers consist of engaging texts in a variety of genres, including fantasy, folk tales, realistic fiction, historical fiction, and narrative and expository nonfiction. To better address real-life reading skills that students will encounter in testing situations and beyond, a higher percentage of nonfiction texts is provided at each grade.

USING THE LEVELED READERS

You can use the leveled readers to meet the diverse needs of your students. Consider using the readers to

- practice critical skills and strategies
- build fluency
- build vocabulary and concepts
- build background for the main selections in the student book
- provide a variety of reading experiences, e.g., shared, group, individual, take-home, readers' theater

GUIDED READING APPROACH

The *Reading Street* leveled readers are leveled according to Guided Reading criteria by experts trained in Guided Reading. The Guided Reading levels increase in difficulty within a grade level and across grade levels. In addition to leveling according to Guided Reading criteria, the instruction provided in the *Leveled Reader Teaching Guide* is compatible with Guided Reading instruction. An instructional routine is provided for each leveled reader. This routine is most effective when working with individual students or small groups.

MANAGING THE CLASSROOM

When using the leveled readers with individuals or small groups, you'll want to keep the other students engaged in meaningful, independent learning tasks. Establishing independent practice stations throughout the classroom and routines for these stations can help you manage the rest of the class while you work with individuals or small groups. Practice stations can include listening, phonics, vocabulary, independent reading, and cross-curricular activities. For classroom management, create a work board that lists the stations and which students should be at each station. Provide instructions at each station that detail the tasks to be accomplished. Update the board and alert students when they should rotate to a new station. For additional support for managing your classroom, see the *Reading Street* Practice Stations' *Classroom Management Handbook.*

USING THE LEVELED READER TEACHING GUIDE

The *Leveled Reader Teaching Guide* provides an instruction plan for each leveled reader based on the same instructional routine.

INTRODUCE THE BOOK The Introduction includes suggestions for creating interest in the text by discussing the title and author, building background, and previewing the book and its features.

READ THE BOOK Before students begin reading the book, have them set purposes for reading and discuss how they can use the reading strategy as they read. Determine how you want students in a particular group to read the text, softly or silently, to a specific point or the entire text. Then use the Comprehension Questions to provide support as needed and to assess comprehension.

REVISIT THE BOOK The Reader Response questions provide opportunities for students to demonstrate their understanding of the text, the target comprehension skill, and vocabulary. The Response Options require students to revisit the text to respond to what they've read and to move beyond the text to explore related content.

SKILL WORK The Skill Work box provides instruction and practice for the target skill and strategy and selection vocabulary. Instruction for an alternate comprehension skill allows teachers to provide additional skill instruction and practice for students.

USING THE GRAPHIC ORGANIZERS

Graphic organizers in blackline-master format can be found on pages 132–152. These can be used as overhead transparencies or as student worksheets.

ASSESSING PERFORMANCE

Use the assessment forms that begin on page 6 to make notes about your students' reading skills, use of reading strategies, and general reading behaviors.

MEASURE FLUENT READING (pp. 6–7) Provides directions for measuring a student's fluency, based on words correct per minute (wcpm), and reading accuracy using a running record.

OBSERVATION CHECKLIST (p. 8) Allows you to note the regularity with which students demonstrate their understanding and use of reading skills and strategies.

STUDENT SELF-ASSESSMENT (p. 9) Helps students identify their own areas of strength and areas where they need further work. This form (About My Reading) encourages them to list steps they can take to become better readers and to set goals as readers. Suggest that students share their self-assessment notes with their families so that family members can work with them more effectively to practice their reading skills and strategies at home.

READING STRATEGY ASSESSMENT (p. 10) Provides criteria for evaluating each student's proficiency as a strategic reader.

PROGRESS REPORT (p. 11) Provides a means to track a student's book-reading progress over a period of time by noting the level at which a student reads and his or her accuracy at that level. Reading the chart from left to right gives you a visual model of how quickly a student is making the transition from one level to the next. Share these reports with parents or guardians to help them see how their child's reading is progressing.

Measure Fluent Reading

Taking a Running Record

A running record is an assessment of a student's oral reading accuracy and oral reading fluency. Reading accuracy is based on the number of words read correctly. Reading fluency is based on the reading rate (the number of words correct per minute) and the degree to which a student reads with a "natural flow."

How to Measure Reading Accuracy

1. Choose a grade-level text of about 80 to 120 words that is unfamiliar to the student.
2. Make a copy of the text for yourself. Make a copy for the student or have the student read aloud from a book.
3. Give the student the text and have the student read aloud. (You may wish to record the student's reading for later evaluation.)
4. On your copy of the text, mark any miscues or errors the student makes while reading. See the running record sample on page 7, which shows how to identify and mark miscues.
5. Count the total number of words in the text and the total number of errors made by the student. Note: If a student makes the same error more than once, such as mispronouncing the same word multiple times, count it as one error. Self-corrections do not count as actual errors. Use the following formula to calculate the percentage score, or accuracy rate:

$$\frac{\text{Total Number of Words} - \text{Total Number of Errors}}{\text{Total Number of Words}} \times 100 = \text{percentage score}$$

Interpreting the Results

- A student who reads **95–100%** of the words correctly is reading at an **independent level** and may need more challenging text.
- A student who reads **90–94%** of the words correctly is reading at an **instructional level** and will likely benefit from guided instruction.
- A student who reads **89%** or fewer of the words correctly is reading at a **frustrational level** and may benefit most from targeted instruction with lower-level texts and intervention.

How to Measure Reading Rate (WCPM)

1. Follow Steps 1–3 above.
2. Note the exact times when the student begins and finishes reading.
3. Use the following formula to calculate the number of words correct per minute (WCPM):

$$\frac{\text{Total Number of Words Read Correctly}}{\text{Total Number of Seconds}} \times 60 = \text{words correct per minute}$$

Interpreting the Results

By the end of the year, a fifth-grader should be reading approximately 130–140 WCPM.

Running Record Sample

Running Record Sample

Did you know that every day in	7
cities across the United States, students	13
just like you are helping others?	19
Each year in Louisiana, a young	25
student and her younger brother have	31
gone around collecting stuffed animals	36
for children who live in a homeless	43
shelter.	44
In New York City, seventy-six	49
students from Harlem teamed up with	55
four Olympic athletes to transform	60
a run-down park into a playground	66
featuring a daffodil garden.	70
And each year in Indiana, a young	77
student has gone around collecting	82
hundreds of bundles of baby clothes	88
and other baby items. In the fall she	96
delivers them to a home for mothers	103
who are having tough times.	108

Annotations: ✓ marks over words; H over "Louisiana"; "the" inserted after "for"; "seventy-six" circled; "each" crossed out with "every" written above; "sc" under "gone"; /tug/ over "tough".

Notations

Accurate Reading
The student reads a word correctly.

Hesitation
The student hesitates over a word, and the teacher provides the word. Wait several seconds before telling the student what the word is.

Insertion
The student inserts words or parts of words that are not in the text.

Omission
The student omits words or word parts.

Substitution
The student substitutes words or parts of words for the words in the text.

Self-correction
The student reads a word incorrectly but then corrects the error. Do not count self-corrections as actual errors. However, noting self-corrections will help you identify words the student finds difficult.

Mispronunciation/Misreading
The student pronounces or reads a word incorrectly.

Running Record Results
Total Number of Words: **108**
Number of Errors: **5**

Reading Time: **51 seconds**

▶ **Reading Accuracy**

$$\frac{108 - 5}{108} \times 100 = 95.370 = 95\%$$

Accuracy Percentage Score: **95%**

▶ **Reading Rate—WCPM**

$$\frac{103}{51} \times 60 = 121.18 = 121 \text{ words correct per minute}$$

Reading Rate: **121 WCPM**

Observation Checklist

Student's Name________________________________ Date__________

Behaviors Observed	Always (Proficient)	Usually (Fluent)	Sometimes (Developing)	Rarely (Novice)
Reading Strategies and Skills				
Uses prior knowledge and preview to understand what book is about				
Makes predictions and checks them while reading				
Uses context clues to figure out meanings of new words				
Uses phonics and syllabication to decode words				
Self-corrects while reading				
Reads at an appropriate reading rate				
Reads with appropriate intonation and stress				
Uses fix-up strategies				
Identifies story elements: character, setting, plot, theme				
Summarizes plot or main ideas accurately				
Uses target comprehension skill to understand the text better				
Responds thoughtfully about the text				
Reading Behaviors and Attitudes				
Enjoys listening to stories				
Chooses reading as a free-time activity				
Reads with sustained interest and attention				
Participates in discussion about books				

General Comments

About My Reading

Name ________________________________ Date __________

1. Compared with earlier in the year, I am enjoying reading

☐ more ☐ less ☐ about the same

2. When I read now, I understand

☐ more than I used to ☐ about the same as I used to

3. One thing that has helped me with my reading is

____

____

____

4. One thing that could make me a better reader is

____

____

____

5. Here is one selection or book that I really enjoyed reading:

____

____

6. Here are some reasons why I liked it:

____

____

____

____

____

____

Reading Strategy Assessment

Student ______________________ Date ______________________

Teacher ______________________

		Proficient	Developing	Emerging	Not showing trait
Building Background Comments:	Previews	☐	☐	☐	☐
	Asks questions	☐	☐	☐	☐
	Predicts	☐	☐	☐	☐
	Activates prior knowledge	☐	☐	☐	☐
	Sets own purposes for reading	☐	☐	☐	☐
	Other:	☐	☐	☐	☐
Comprehension Comments:	Retells/summarizes	☐	☐	☐	☐
	Questions, evaluates ideas	☐	☐	☐	☐
	Relates to self/other texts	☐	☐	☐	☐
	Paraphrases	☐	☐	☐	☐
	Rereads/reads ahead for meaning	☐	☐	☐	☐
	Visualizes	☐	☐	☐	☐
	Uses decoding strategies	☐	☐	☐	☐
	Uses vocabulary strategies	☐	☐	☐	☐
	Understands key ideas of a text	☐	☐	☐	☐
	Other:	☐	☐	☐	☐
Fluency Comments:	Adjusts reading rate	☐	☐	☐	☐
	Reads for accuracy	☐	☐	☐	☐
	Uses expression	☐	☐	☐	☐
	Other:	☐	☐	☐	☐
Connections Comments:	Relates text to self	☐	☐	☐	☐
	Relates text to text	☐	☐	☐	☐
	Relates text to world	☐	☐	☐	☐
	Other:	☐	☐	☐	☐
Self-Assessment Comments:	Is aware of: Strengths	☐	☐	☐	☐
	Needs	☐	☐	☐	☐
	Improvement/achievement	☐	☐	☐	☐
	Sets and implements learning goals	☐	☐	☐	☐
	Maintains logs, records, portfolio	☐	☐	☐	☐
	Works with others	☐	☐	☐	☐
	Shares ideas and materials	☐	☐	☐	☐
	Other:	☐	☐	☐	☐

Progress Report

Student's Name ______________________________

At the top of the chart, record the book title, its grade/unit/week (for example, 1.2.3), and the student's accuracy percentage. See page 6 for measuring fluency, calculating accuracy and reading rates. At the bottom of the chart, record the date you took the running record. In the middle of the chart, make an X in the box across from the level of the student's reading—frustrational level (below 89% accuracy), instructional level (90–94% accuracy), or independent level (95–100% accuracy). Record the reading rate (WCPM) in the next row.

Book Title							
Grade/Unit/Week							
Reading Accuracy Percentage							
LEVEL	**Frustrational** (89% or below)						
	Instructional (90–94%)						
	Independent (95% or above)						
Reading Rate (WCPM)							
Date							

The Long Trip Home

5.1.1

CHARACTER AND PLOT
MONITOR AND CLARIFY

SUMMARY In this fiction story, Jake is angry with his parents for missing yet another one of his soccer games. When he and his uncle are stranded on an isolated country road on the way home from the game, Jake confronts his fears and emotions. As he journeys with his uncle toward home, he also journeys toward a new appreciation of himself and his parents.

LESSON VOCABULARY

compressed	grumbled
insistently	intentionally
minute	neutral
normally	

INTRODUCE THE BOOK

INTRODUCE THE TITLE AND AUTHOR Discuss with students the title and the author of *The Long Road Home*. Ask students to tell what they think the book will be about, based on the title and the cover illustration.

BUILD BACKGROUND Invite students to talk about a time when they had to confront their fears. Invite them to talk about the experience and what they learned from it. Ask students how the experience changed them.

PREVIEW/USE TEXT FEATURES Have students preview the book by looking at the illustrations. Ask students to discuss how these text features give an idea of what this book will be about. Ask where they think the road in the pictures is located.

READ THE BOOK

SET PURPOSE Have students set a purpose for reading *The Long Trip Home*. Ask: What road do you think the author is talking about? Is she talking about a physical road?

STRATEGY SUPPORT: MONITOR AND CLARIFY Have students *monitor and clarify* their understanding as they read by taking notes. Have them write down each major event that occurs to Jake in the story as he and Uncle Dave make their way home to the cabin. Encourage them to ask questions when they are confused.

COMPREHENSION QUESTIONS

PAGE 3 Why isn't Jake more excited about his team winning the soccer game? *(His parents weren't there to see him score the winning goal.)*

PAGE 8 What do you predict will happen after the car hits the tree? Why? *(Responses will vary, but should be supported by details from the story.)*

PAGES 10–14 What are some things that Uncle Dave does to help calm Jake's fears? *(remains calm; gives Jake a flashlight; gives Jake his jacket; makes jokes; takes Jake's fears seriously and gives him rational explanations)*

PAGE 22 How did Jake's parents react when Jake finally reached the house? *(They hugged him and told him they'd try never to miss one of his games again.)*

REVISIT THE BOOK

READER RESPONSE

1. Possible answer: At first, he was angry that his parents missed his game. He was afraid of the dark roads and having to walk home through the woods. In the end, he was proud of himself and happy that his parents were proud of him too.
2. Responses will vary.
3. The base words are *insistent, intention,* and *normal*. Sentences will vary.
4. Responses will vary.

EXTEND UNDERSTANDING Have students comment on the illustrations in this story. Ask: Which ones do you like best? What details about the characters are shown in the illustrations? How would you have portrayed the characters differently?

RESPONSE OPTIONS

WRITING Invite students to write a paragraph about a time when they learned something positive about themselves. Ask them to write about what they learned and how they felt at the time.

SCIENCE CONNECTION

TIME FOR Science

Have students research wildlife found in rural Maine using the library or the Internet. Ask them to make a list of animals that they learn about.

Skill Work

TEACH/REVIEW VOCABULARY

Invite students to use each of the vocabulary words in a sentence. Challenge them to write sentences related to the selection.

TARGET SKILL AND STRATEGY

CHARACTER AND PLOT Remind students that a *character* is a person who takes part in the events of a story. Readers can often determine character traits based on a character's actions, thoughts, feelings, and words. The *plot* is an organized sequence of events. Explain that authors sometimes use flashbacks, in which the action of the story is interrupted to talk about something that happened in the past. Foreshadowing is another technique, in which the writer hints at events to come in the story. Challenge students to note character traits and to find examples of flashbacks and foreshadowing in this book.

ELL Help students brainstorm words that describe characters, such as *confident, scared, brave, lonely, friendly, caring*. Invite students to write a description of a character from the story using words from the list.

MONITOR AND CLARIFY Remind students to *monitor*, or check, whether they understand what they read. Tell them that if they do not understand something, one way to *clarify* is to make a quick summary of the details they have just read. Suggest that understanding what they read will help them determine the author's purpose for writing. At the end of each page or main event, students should ask themselves: What is the author trying to tell me here?

ADDITIONAL SKILL INSTRUCTION

PROBLEM AND SOLUTION Explain to students that a *problem*, or conflict, is usually introduced at the beginning of a story and may be between two people or two groups of people, between a person and a force of nature, or within a person. The *solution* to the problem comes at the end of the story. The problem is solved, the action winds down, and the story ends. Ask students to identify two problems Jake faces, and the solutions to these problems.

Name ______________________

Character and Plot

- A **character** is a person who takes part in the events of a story.
- The **plot** is an organized sequence of events. Authors often use flashbacks to tell about something that has already happened and foreshadowing to hint at events to come.

Directions Fill in the graphic organizer to tell about *The Long Trip Home*. Under Events, include flashback and foreshadowing.

Title ______________________

Characters

Setting

Problem

Events

Solution

Name ___________________________________

Vocabulary

Directions Read each sentence. Write the word from the box that has the same meaning as the underlined word or phrase.

Check the Words You Know

___**compressed**
___**insistently**
___**minute**
___**normally**
___**grumbled**
___**intentionally**
___**neutral**

1. Jake muttered in discontent when Uncle Dave tried to cheer him up.

____

2. Uncle Dave purposely took the service road. ___________________________

3. Uncle Dave's car was squeezed against a tree after the accident. ___________________________

4. It took a short time for Uncle Dave to respond to Jake. ___________________________

5. Jake spoke repeatedly and urgently to Uncle Dave. ___________________________

6. Although Jake was angry with his parents, Uncle Dave remained unbiased.

____

7. Uncle Dave acted in a usual way throughout the trip through the woods.

____

Directions Write a summary of *The Long Trip Home,* using as many vocabulary words as possible.

____

____

____

____

____

____

____

____

Storm Chasing Challenges

5.1.2

CAUSE AND EFFECT
SUMMARIZE

SUMMARY In Tornado Alley, which crosses the plains of the United States, storm chasers track tornadoes to learn more about them and to experience the thrill of seeing them up close. But storm chasing can be dangerous, especially when practiced by novice chasers.

LESSON VOCABULARY

branded	constructed
daintily	devastation
lullaby	pitch
resourceful	thieving
veins	

INTRODUCE THE BOOK

INTRODUCE THE TITLE AND AUTHOR Discuss with students the title and the author of *Storm Chasing Challenges*. Have students discuss the challenges they expect to read about.

BUILD BACKGROUND Ask students whether they have ever seen a tornado in real life, on TV, or in a movie. Ask them to describe what they have seen. Ask: What other types of storms have you seen up close?

ELL Students may be familiar with countries that do not have tornadoes. Show students photographs of tornadoes to help them visualize this type of storm. Encourage them to describe a tornado and the kinds of damage it can do.

PREVIEW/USE TEXT FEATURES Have students preview the book by looking at the photographs, the map on pages 4–5, and the diagrams on pages 10 and 13. Ask: What do you think you will learn from this book?

READ THE BOOK

SET PURPOSE Ask students to set a purpose for reading *Storm Chasing Challenges*. Ideas might include to learn about the tools of storm chasers, to learn how storm chasers find tornadoes, and to understand the dangers of storm chasing.

STRATEGY SUPPORT: SUMMARIZE Remind students that to *summarize* means to briefly tell what happened in a story. Have students review the main ideas that they wrote down. Ask them to write a short summary of the entire book, based on their notes of the most important parts.

COMPREHENSION QUESTIONS

PAGE 5 What are some of the goals of a storm chaser? *(to study weather patterns and meteorology and to experience the thrill of seeing a tornado up close)*

PAGE 7 What are some popular storm-tracking tools? *(radar, laptop computers, video cameras, radios, satellite images)*

PAGE 9 What effect do "renegade" storm chasers have on others? *(They make roads more dangerous by speeding; they risk their own lives and the lives of others.)*

PAGES 12–13 What makes a tornado funnel? *(Cold air moves over warm air. Then lighter air rises up through cold air, creating the funnel cloud, which rotates.)*

PAGE 15 What were the effects of the May 1999 Oklahoma tornado? *(It destroyed houses and neighborhoods around Oklahoma City.)*

PAGE 19 How and when did storm chasing begin? *(In the 1950s, a North Dakota man followed storms and photographed them.)*

REVISIT THE BOOK

READER RESPONSE

1. Tornado Alley has many storms in the spring because of weather patterns that occur during that time of year. This makes spring the best season to spot tornadoes, but a dangerous time as well.
2. Responses will vary. Responses should reflect the main idea from each section and then summarize the general concept of the book as a whole.
3. *brand, construct;* sentences will vary.
4. Responses will vary. Students should know which states are part of Tornado Alley and where it is located in the U.S.

EXTEND UNDERSTANDING Encourage students to discuss why the photographs and diagrams are such an integral part of the book. Ask: Without the photos, would you have enjoyed this book as much? What did the photos and diagrams help you learn?

RESPONSE OPTIONS

WRITING Have students prepare a list of things they would do or not do in order to remain safe during a tornado.

SCIENCE CONNECTION

TIME FOR Science

Have students research Hurricane Hunters, people who fly into the eye of a hurricane to study it. Invite students to go to the library or use the Internet for their research.

Skill Work

TEACH/REVIEW VOCABULARY

After you review the meanings of the vocabulary words with students, call on volunteers to use each word in a sentence.

TARGET SKILL AND STRATEGY

CAUSE AND EFFECT Remind students that a *cause* is why something happened; the *effect* is what happened. Note that sometimes a cause may have multiple effects, and an effect may have more than one cause. Encourage students to pose questions to themselves as they read, such as: What happened? What caused it to happen? This will work especially well when students read about tornadoes and look at photo on pages 14–15.

SUMMARIZE Remind students that to summarize means to briefly tell what happened in a book. Have students list the main ideas in the story as they read.

ADDITIONAL SKILL INSTRUCTION

DRAW CONCLUSIONS Remind students that a *conclusion* is a sensible decision reached after you have thought about details or facts you have read. *Drawing conclusions* is the process of making those sensible decisions. After students have finished reading the text, looking at the photos, and studying the diagrams, have them draw conclusions about the dangers of tornadoes.

Name_______________________________________

Cause and Effect

- A **cause** is the reason something happens. The **effect** is what happens.
- A cause may have more than one effect, and an effect may have more than one cause.
- Sometimes a cause is not directly stated, and you need to think about why something happened.

Directions Read the following passage. Then answer the questions that follow.

Tornadoes form when a layer of cold air moves over a layer of warm air. The lighter air rises up through the cold air. This makes the funnel cloud rotate as the air changes places. A tornado can do amazing damage to buildings, property, and land. Tornado winds, rising to a furious pitch, will rip through a town, and destroy everything in their path. Houses and mobile homes may be flattened, ripped apart, or carried away completely. A tornado can even peel the bark off trees!

But as dangerous as they are, tornadoes are a great source of delight for storm chasers. They love to seek out, or chase, tornadoes. Their task is a dangerous one. High winds can flip the chaser's vehicle or blow out car windows. Heavy rain and hail can make it hard to see. Flooding and fog can make traveling harder and might strand a chaser in the path of a storm. Lightning, a release of electricity in the atmosphere, is another danger for storm chasers. It can strike without warning!

1. Describe the cause of tornadoes.

____

____

2. What are two effects of tornadoes?

____

____

3. What is the cause for lightning, as stated in the passage?

____

____

4. What are two effects of tornadoes on storm chasers?

____

____

5. Would you like to be a storm chaser? Why or why not? Give examples from the reader to support your choice.

____

____

Name ____

Vocabulary

Directions Write the vocabulary word that best matches each definition below. One word, with two different meanings, is used twice.

Check the Words You Know

___branded	___constructed	___daintily
___devastation	___lullaby	___pitch
___resourceful	___thieving	___veins

1. the act of laying waste, destroying ____________________
2. likely to steal ____________________
3. with delicate beauty ____________________
4. thick, black, sticky substance made from tar ____________________
5. soft song sung to put a baby to sleep ____________________
6. good at thinking of ways to do things ____________________
7. marked by burning ____________________
8. tubes that carry blood through your body ____________________
9. put together ____________________

Directions Choose two vocabulary words and use each in a sentence below.

10. ____

____

11. ____

____

Toby's California Vacation

5.1.3

SETTING AND THEME
INFERRING

SUMMARY This story is about a boy named Toby who visits the Channel Islands off the California coast with his family. Toby learns about the unique plants and animals on each island and the importance of respecting nature.

LESSON VOCABULARY

gnawed	headland
kelp	lair
ravine	shellfish
sinew	

INTRODUCE THE BOOK

INTRODUCE THE TITLE AND AUTHOR Discuss with students the title and the author of *Toby's California Vacation*. Based on the cover photo, ask students to describe the image they get of what the book will be about.

BUILD BACKGROUND Discuss what students know about endangered species. Ask them to name animals they can think of that are endangered, like the spotted owl. Prompt them to discuss reasons why these animals are endangered.

PREVIEW/USE TEXT FEATURES As students preview the book, ask them to look at the photographs and read the captions. Based on these features, ask students what they think the book will be about. Draw their attention to the photographs on pages 10–11. Ask them what they think the book will tell them about these animals.

READ THE BOOK

SET PURPOSE Have students set a purpose for reading *Toby's California Vacation*. Prompt them to think about the importance of preserving our environment and taking care of plants and animals.

STRATEGY SUPPORT: INFERRING Remind students that *inferring* is taking facts and details you read and making a guess about information that the author didn't mention. Have students read through page 11 noting the questions. Ask them to infer what other information Toby would want to know such as what specific animals or plants are found in the Channel Islands.

COMPREHENSION QUESTIONS

PAGE 5 How many islands make up the Channel Islands and where are they located? *(eight islands, four northern and four southern)*

PAGE 11 What is the setting? *(Santa Cruz Island)*

PAGE 11 What words or phrases on this page help you visualize the setting? *(largest island, mountain ranges, ravines, tide pools, sea caves, deer, mice, many reptiles, sea lions)*

PAGE 20 Why is Alcatraz famous? *(It used to have a prison where dangerous criminals were held.)*

REVISIT THE BOOK

READER RESPONSE

1. San Diego; palm trees, big buildings, wide roads, beaches, ocean.
2. Possible responses: enthusiastic, curious, outgoing. Responses will vary.
3. Responses will vary; a point of land extending out into water.
4. Possible responses: cleaning up trash, not polluting, recycling, walking instead of driving.

EXTEND UNDERSTANDING Discuss with students one of the themes of this story, such as the importance of helping endangered species. Ask students how this theme affects them. Prompt them to think about ways the threat of animal extinction affects Earth and its people.

RESPONSE OPTIONS

WRITING Suggest students imagine what it would be like to visit one of the Channel Islands. Have them write a short description of the experience, using vivid details.

SOCIAL STUDIES CONNECTION

Time For SOCIAL STUDIES

Students can learn more about endangered animals by researching them on the Internet or in the library. Suggest that they choose an endangered animal that interests them most and read about ways people are trying to preserve them. Encourage students to get involved in some way, such as having a bake sale to raise money or writing a letter to the government asking for help.

Skill Work

TEACH/REVIEW VOCABULARY

Have students look up each word in a dictionary and write the definitions on a sheet of paper. Then have volunteers write a sentence using a vocabulary word you've written on the board. Repeat this until all words are used.

ELL Have students write each vocabulary word on one side of an index card and its definition on the back. Then have students take turns reading the definitions and guessing which words go with them.

TARGET SKILL AND STRATEGY

SETTING AND THEME Remind students that *setting* is the time and place in which a story occurs. As students read, ask them to write down the setting of the story and have them ask themselves: Does the theme depend on the setting of the story? Remind students that *theme* is the underlying meaning of a story, a "big idea" that stands on its own outside a story. As students read, have them answer the following question: What does the writer want me to learn or know from reading this story?

INFERRING Review that *inferring* means to make a guess about the story from evidence and reasoning rather than from direct statements by the author. Remind students that understanding the actions of a character can help *infer* something about his or her personality and future actions. For example, throughout this story, Toby is constantly asking questions. Students can use this information to infer something about his personality. After reading the story, ask students to infer whether or not Toby was a good student in school. What helped them infer this?

ADDITIONAL SKILL INSTRUCTION

GENERALIZE Remind students that sometimes they are given ideas about several things or people in a text that they can make a statement about as a group. This statement is called a *generalization*. Valid generalizations are accurate or true. As students read, have them make generalizations about each island. Ask them to list facts to support their generalizations.

Name ____________________

Setting and Theme

- **Setting** is the time and place in which the story occurs.
- **Theme** is the subject or idea of a story.

Directions Based on your understanding of *Toby's California Vacation*, answer the questions below.

1. What is the setting of the story?

____

____

2. What is the story's theme?

____

____

____

3. Does the theme depend on the setting of the story? Why or why not?

____

____

____

4. What is another setting where the theme of the story would still be the same? Why?

____

____

____

Name ____________________________

Vocabulary

Directions Write the vocabulary word that matches each definition.

Check the Words You Know

___gnawed
___kelp
___ravine
___sinew
___headland
___lair
___shellfish

1. a type of seaweed ____________________
2. chewed ____________________
3. a sea animal that has a shell ____________________
4. gully ____________________
5. a vein ____________________
6. a point of land extending out into water ____________________
7. den or home ____________________

Directions Write three sentences, using as many vocabulary words as you can.

8. ____
____
9. ____
____
10. ____
____

Famous Women in Sports

5.1.4

FACT AND OPINION
ASK QUESTIONS

SUMMARY This book highlights women who have broken gender and race barriers in the field of sports.

LESSON VOCABULARY

confidence	fastball
mocking	outfield
unique	weakness
windup	

INTRODUCE THE BOOK

INTRODUCE THE TITLE AND AUTHOR Discuss with students the title and the author of *Famous Women in Sports*. Have students look at the cover and ask them what they think they might learn from this book. What tells them that this will be a nonfiction book? (the Biography label in the upper right corner) Does the photo peak students' interest in the book and make them want to read more? Why or why not?

BUILD BACKGROUND Invite students to name famous women athletes. Ask them whether they think women in the past had the same opportunity to play sports as men. What are they basing their knowledge on? Do they think that girls and women today have the same athletic opportunities as boys and men?

PREVIEW/USE TEXT FEATURES Have students look at the features in the book before reading. What kind of art is used? *(photos)* Why do they think photos are used in this book? Point out the headings. What can students learn from the headings? *(the names of the women and their sports)* Remind them that reading the captions will give them important information about the women.

READ THE BOOK

SET PURPOSE Have students set a purpose for reading *Famous Women in Sports*. Students' interest in sports, women's sports, and history should determine this purpose. Remind students that women's sports have changed over the years. Suggest that students think about why that happened and who helped make those changes.

STRATEGY SUPPORT: ASK QUESTIONS Revisit how asking questions before and during reading can help keep the reader engaged with the text. Then discuss how asking questions after reading can also help students check comprehension and solidify what they've learned. For example: *What did I learn about women's sports that I didn't know before?*

COMPREHENSION QUESTIONS

PAGE 5 How many times did Trudy attempt to swim the English Channel? *(two)*

PAGES 8–9 What questions does the information on these pages answer about women and baseball? *(Responses will vary.)*

PAGES 16–18 How was Rosemary Casals different than other women tennis players? *(Possible response: Hispanic, poor, wore colorful clothes)*

PAGE 18 Which two women worked together for the rights of female tennis players? *(Rosemary Casals and Billy Jean King)*

REVISIT THE BOOK

READER RESPONSE

1. Possible responses:
   Babe Didrickson—fact—won two gold medals for track and field in the 1932 Olympics; opinion—was never afraid to speak her mind
   Althea Gibson—fact—became the first African American to play at Wimbledon; opinion—unique athlete who broke through many barriers
   Billie Jean King—fact—first female athlete to win more than $100,000 in annual prize money; opinion—King's win over Bobby Riggs proved that women could excel at sports too.
   Rosemary Casals—fact—in 1966, Casals started playing in doubles tournaments with Billie Jean King; opinion—she energized the sport of tennis
2. Possible responses: why women are not allowed to run the Boston Marathon; why does the official think he can drag Switzer out of the race once she started. Asking questions helps the reader consider the background and history of women in sports.
3. Possible responses: *universe, unit, uniform;* sentences will vary.
4. Responses will vary.

EXTEND UNDERSTANDING Discuss the following with students: What kinds of photos are in this book? Are they mostly action shots or of people standing still? How do these photos help you understand the written text? Have students each pick a photo and describe in their own words what they see.

RESPONSE OPTIONS

WRITING/VIEWING Challenge students to design promotional posters for one of the sporting events mentioned in this book.

SOCIAL STUDIES CONNECTION

Time For SOCIAL STUDIES

Have students pick one of the women from this book or any accomplished female sports figure. Ask them to use class books, the library, or the Internet to find out more information on their subject. Encourage students to discuss why they picked a particular person.

Skill Work

TEACH/REVIEW VOCABULARY

Divide the group into teams. Play a quick game where students take turns giving definitions of the words while the rest of the team guesses the words. Whichever team guesses the correct word first, wins.

ELL Students might not be familiar with some of the sports terminology. Review *outfield, windup,* and *fastball,* as well as *croquet,* and *badminton* (page 3), and *bunt* (page 8).

TARGET SKILL AND STRATEGY

FACT AND OPINION Remind students that a statement of *fact* is a statement that can be proven true or false, and a statement of *opinion* is someone's judgment. A statement of opinion cannot be proven true or false. Have students point out statements of fact and opinion they find as they read the book *Famous Women in Sports*.

ASK QUESTIONS Review that *asking questions* before, during, and after reading will help students focus and comprehend the text. Students can generate questions to help them focus on and keep track of the sequence of events that take place in the history of women's sports. Tell students that as they read, they should write down a couple of questions they want answered. For example, when they get to the section on women's baseball, they might ask: *When was the first women's baseball league established? What events caused the league to finally shut down?*

ADDITIONAL SKILL INSTRUCTION

COMPARE AND CONTRAST Remind students that to *compare and contrast* things means to look for how they are alike and different. Students can compare information in the book to their own knowledge; they should also pay attention to the comparisons and contrasts that the author makes. Tell students that as they read, they can compare women's sports of the past to what they know of women's sports today.

Name ____

Fact and Opinion

- A statement of **fact** can be proven true or false by reading, observing, or asking an expert.
- A statement of **opinion** is a judgment or belief. It cannot be proven true or false but can be supported or explained.

Directions Read the following passage. Decide which sentences are statements of fact and which sentences are statements of opinion. Then complete the chart below.

In the 1800s women were allowed to play very few organized sports. By the beginning of the 1900s, change was in the air. One female athlete was Mildred Didrikson. She was given the nickname "Babe" because people thought she played baseball as well as Babe Ruth. Babe won two gold medals for track and field in the 1932 Olympics. She would have won a third but was disqualified by the high jump judges. They disqualified her because they though her style of diving headfirst over the bar was inappropriate! Didrikson died in 1956. She is still remembered as one of the greatest athletes ever, male or female.

Statements of Fact	Statements of Opinion

Name ____

Vocabulary

Directions Which vocabulary words are compound words? Write a definition for each word you list.

Check the Words You Know

___confidence	___fastball	___mocking
___outfield	___unique	___weakness
___windup		

1. ______________________________

____

____

____

____

____

Directions Match each of the words to its antonym, or opposite meaning.

2. confidence — strength

3. unique — ordinary

4. weakness — doubt

Directions Write the definition for the word *mocking*.

5. ______________________________

____

Directions Choose three vocabulary words and use each in a sentence below.

6. ____

____

7. ____

____

8. ____

____

A Railroad Over the Sierra

5.1.5

CAUSE AND EFFECT
TEXT STRUCTURE

SUMMARY This book explores the building of the first transcontinental railroad. It tells of the obstacles the railroad industry faced while constructing the railroad line, as well as the hardships Chinese immigrant workers endured while working towards its completion.

LESSON VOCABULARY

barren	deafening	lurched
previous	prying	surveying

INTRODUCE THE BOOK

INTRODUCE THE TITLE AND AUTHOR Discuss with students the title and the author of *A Railroad Over the Sierra*. Based on the title and cover art, ask students to describe what they think this book is about.

BUILD BACKGROUND Ask students what they know about immigration and immigrants. If any of the students in the class are immigrants, encourage them to share their experience—what it was like to move, to live in a new environment, to learn a new culture. If nobody has had such an experience, a parallel discussion can include moving from one city or state to another.

PREVIEW/USE ILLUSTRATIONS Have students skim through the book, looking at the photographs and illustrations. Ask: What do you think the book is about? Who are some important people in this history? What main topics does the book appear to focus on?

READ THE BOOK

SET PURPOSE Have students set a purpose for reading *A Railroad Over the Sierra*. This purpose should be guided by the impressions they get from reading the title and skimming the photographs, illustrations, and captions, along with their own curiosity.

STRATEGY SUPPORT: TEXT STRUCTURE Remind students that *story structure* describes the arrangement of a fictional story, while *text structure* refers to the way an author organizes information in a nonfiction book. Guide students to see that this book is organized chronologically, or in sequence, and that each chapter defines a different aspect of the railroad's construction.

COMPREHENSION QUESTIONS

PAGE 5 What was the plan for building the transcontinental railroad? *(Central Pacific would build east from Sacramento, and Union Pacific would build west from Nebraska.)*

PAGE 6 What was a major obstacle in building the railroad? *(The railway needed to build through the Sierra Nevada to get across the California border into Nevada.)*

PAGES 11–12 What were some lifestyle differences between Chinese workers and white workers? *(Chinese workers were paid less; they had to provide their own food; they slept in tents while white workers slept in railroad cars; they ate different food that kept them healthy; they didn't waste their money; they kept themselves clean.)*

PAGE 16 What was the danger of working in the mountains? *(Nitroglycerine charges could explode without warning while they were being set; the explosions themselves were dangerous; winter was long with lots of snow; explosions caused avalanches.)*

REVISIT THE BOOK

READER RESPONSE

1. White workers were unreliable because they often left to prospect for gold, or they caused trouble. It was difficult to find enough workers to do the work. Crocker hired a small number of Chinese immigrants, who proved to be reliable, strong, and smart. Soon he hired as many Chinese workers as he could get.
2. Responses will vary but preparation explanations should generally state that headings indicated what the section would be about.
3. Responses will vary.
4. Responses will vary, but answers should be supported with evidence from the text. Arguments should also be supported with details.

EXTEND UNDERSTANDING Remind students that text is structured in many ways to present ideas, such as *chronologically*. Text presented in chronological order shows how elements change over time and also how one event may cause another. Invite students to create their own graphic device that relates information from the book, such as a time line or a cause-and-effect chart. Encourage students to draw conclusions based on the changes they may uncover in their list. For example, they may conclude that, historically, life was difficult for these early Chinese immigrants.

RESPONSE OPTIONS

WRITING Ask students to imagine their family has just immigrated to the United States from China, and that they were hired to work on the transcontinental railroad. Have students think about details such as the condition of their lives and how they feel about the way they are treated. Ask students to write imaginary letters to their relatives back in China. The letters should show how they feel about their new homes and work. Volunteers can read their letters aloud to the class.

SOCIAL STUDIES CONNECTION

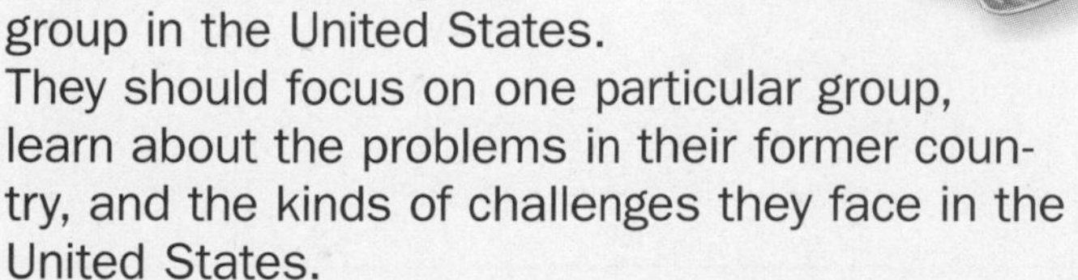

Ask students to research the life of an immigrant group in the United States. They should focus on one particular group, learn about the problems in their former country, and the kinds of challenges they face in the United States.

Skill Work

TEACH/REVIEW VOCABULARY

Read the vocabulary words. Ask students about words they may already know. Discuss how they first heard of the words and what they think the words mean. Tell them that they will become more familiar with these words as they read.

TARGET SKILL AND STRATEGY

CAUSE AND EFFECT Remind students that an *effect* is something that happens, and a *cause* is why something happens. Give students a pair of sentences related to the subject of this book that show cause and effect, such as: *Facing limited job prospects and an uncertain future in their country, Chinese families sometimes tried to leave and to start a better life in the United States. As a result, the United States is a nation of immigrants.* Have students identify which of these sentences shows a cause and which shows an effect.

TEXT STRUCTURE Remind students that the *structure* of a book is the pattern that helps organize its information. Discuss how this book has been divided into chapters. Ask: By reading the chapter titles, what can you tell about how this book is organized? What do the chapter titles tell you about what the author's purpose might be?

ADDITIONAL SKILL INSTRUCTION

GRAPHIC SOURCES Review with students that *graphic sources* are visual representations of information that can improve their understanding of the text before, during, and after reading. Graphic sources in this text include pictures with captions, a map, and photographs, illustrations, and political cartoons from the era. As they read, ask students how the map on page 5 helps them better understand the text.

Name ___________________________

Cause and Effect

- A **cause** tells why something happened.
- An **effect** tells what happened.

Directions Using the graphic organizer, list three causes and three effects of using Chinese immigrants on the transcontinental railroad. One cause and one effect are done for you.

Causes	Effects
Chinese workers were skillful at using handtools, such as drills and hammers.	
	Chinese immigrants were given more responsibility and heavier work.

Name ____________________________________

Vocabulary

Directions Choose the word from the box that best matches each definition. Write the word on the line.

Check the Words You Know

___barren	___deafening	___lurched
___previous	___prying	___surveying

1. being unpleasantly curious ____________
2. lunged forward ____________
3. extremely loud ____________
4. measuring Earth's surface using mathematics and tools ____________
5. having few trees and little vegetation ____________
6. coming or going before ____________

Directions Choose three vocabulary words and use each in a sentence below.

7. ____

____

8. ____

____

9. ____

____

Sea Life

COMPARE AND CONTRAST
VISUALIZE

SUMMARY The seas are home to many forms of life. Different kinds of sea creatures live in different parts of the oceans. From intertidal regions to coral reefs to hydrothermal vents, this book introduces readers to sea life.

LESSON VOCABULARY

algae	concealed
driftwood	hammock
lamented	sea urchins
sternly	tweezers

INTRODUCE THE BOOK

INTRODUCE THE TITLE AND AUTHOR Discuss with students the title and the author of *Sea Life*. Based on the title, ask students to say what they think the book will be about. Have them examine the cover photograph of the book.

BUILD BACKGROUND Ask students to say whether they have ever been to the sea. Have them describe what happens when the tide comes in and goes out. Have them describe different sea animals that live at the shore's edge. Have them list other sea environments they know. Ask them to say how different kinds of sea environments might be home to different sea animals and why.

ELL Have students who have never been to the ocean conduct interviews with students who have. Help students form questions and answers. Encourage students to ask questions that draw on the five senses: What does the ocean sound like? What does the air smell like? What does ocean water taste like? What does the sand feel like? What do sea creatures at the shore look like?

PREVIEW/USE TEXT FEATURES As students preview the book, invite them to notice the photos and captions. Ask them to say how these text features help the reader understand the information in the book.

READ THE BOOK

SET PURPOSE Have students set a purpose for reading *Sea Life*. Students' interest in where life is found in different parts of the sea should guide this purpose. Ask students to think about sea life along coasts, in coral reefs, and on the ocean floor. How do sea creatures in these different regions differ?

STRATEGY SUPPORT: VISUALIZE Invite students to read the third paragraph on page 6. Ask: Which detail appeals to the sense of sight? *(can cling tightly to rocks using suction);* sound? *(crashing waves)* Ask: How does the use of sensory details help support the main idea in this paragraph? *(Sea stars and mussels are found in both the high tide zone and the mid-tide zone.)*

COMPREHENSION QUESTIONS

PAGE 5 What are the four zones of the intertidal region? *(splash, high tide, mid-tide, low tide)*

PAGE 6 Compare and contrast sea stars and mussels. *(They are found in both the high tide and mid-tide zones. When the tide goes out, mussels close their shells tight, and sea stars cling tightly to rocks.)*

PAGE 10 Why do scientists sometimes call coral reefs the ocean's rain forest? *(because they support such a great diversity of sea life)*

PAGE 12 What detail supports the main idea that camouflage helps some fish stay concealed in the coral? *(Their colors blend with the color of the sand.)*

PAGE 15 What details support the main idea that corals behave differently in the day and in the night? *(Day: retract and protect themselves from predators; night: stretch out and catch food)*

PAGE 17 Which creatures cover themselves with sand? *(clams, sea worms, stingrays, flat fish)*

REVISIT THE BOOK

READER RESPONSE

1. Possible responses: Coral Reefs: found in shallow, tropical waters; areas of tremendous diversity and abundant sea life
   Intertidal Regions: located on the ocean's shores in between tides; shores get wet during high tide and dry out during low tide; divided into four zones
   Both: found in the ocean; home to a wide range of plant and animal life
2. Possible response: At high tide there is not much to see except crabs. At low tide more creatures are visible, from sea urchins to nudibranchs.
3. Possible responses: sea anemones, mussels; sea urchins; scorpion fish; stonefish; octopus; eels
4. Possible response: by types of sea creatures, by geographical locations around the world, by oceans

EXTEND UNDERSTANDING Invite students to point out their favorite text feature. Ask them to say what information they learn from the feature and how it supports the text on the page. Have them explain how the text feature adds to the text.

RESPONSE OPTIONS

WRITING Invite students to compare and contrast two sea animals described in the text. Have them write a paragraph telling how the animals are alike and how they are different.

SCIENCE CONNECTION

Time for Science

Students can learn more about hydrothermal vents and the sea life found around them by going to the library or using the Internet. Have them research scientists who are exploring these deep sea places and the forms of life found there. Ask them why these forms of life are considered so important. Have them tell their findings to the class.

Skill Work

TEACH/REVIEW VOCABULARY

To reinforce the contextual meaning of the word *tweezers,* have students read the last paragraph on page 5. Ask: What words help you understand the meaning of the word *tweezers?* Continue in a similar fashion with the other vocabulary words.

TARGET SKILL AND STRATEGY

COMPARE AND CONTRAST Remind students that to *compare* is to tell how two or more things are alike. To *contrast* is to tell how two or more things are different. Tell students that as they read, they should think about the many kinds of life found in the sea. How are some types of sea life alike and different? In which parts of the ocean do they live? Do they need a lot of sunlight, or can they live in darkness?

VISUALIZE Remind students that to *visualize* is to create a picture in the mind as you read. Authors use images and sensory details to help readers visualize people, places, and things. Explain that images are word pictures. Sensory details appeal to one of the five senses: sight, hearing, smell, touch, or taste. Invite students to look for images and sensory details as they read. Ask them to draw a conclusion about why the author uses images and sensory details to convey information.

ADDITIONAL SKILL INSTRUCTION

MAIN IDEA AND DETAILS Remind students that the *main idea* is the most important idea about a topic. A main idea may be stated at the beginning, middle, or end of a section. Sometimes, however, the main idea is not stated. In this case, readers must infer, or put into their own words, the main idea. As students read each section, have them jot down notes about what they think is the main idea. Have them also jot down *details* that support the main idea of each section. Ask them to look for images or sensory details that help them visualize the main idea.

Name ______________________________

Compare and Contrast

- To **compare** is to tell how two or more things are alike.
- To **contrast** is to tell how two or more things are different.

Directions Read the two paragraphs below. Compare and contrast the tide zones described. Then answer the questions.

The Splash Zone

Animals and plants that live in the splash zone only get wet from waves splashing on them during high tide. Most of the time this area is dry. Only a few sea creatures live here. Black lichens are plants that live on rocks in the splash zone. In the splash zone you might also see varieties of snails, such as black periwinkles and limpets.

High Tide Zone

The high tide zone is wetter than the splash zone. It gets fully soaked twice a day during high tide, but it still dries up. Sea life in the high tide zone must be able to live out of the water for much of the day.

Crabs can live on dry land for hours. They use their strong claws to hang on to slippery rocks. They also use their claws like tweezers to pull food from cracks in the rocks.

1. What characteristics do the splash zone and the high tide zone have in common?

____

____

2. How is the high tide zone different from the splash zone?

____

____

3. What plants and animals can you find in the splash zone?

____

____

4. What must sea life living in the high tide zone be able to do?

____

____

Name____

Vocabulary

Directions Read the sentences below. Write the word from the box that has the same meaning as the underlined word or phrase.

Check the Words You Know

___algae	___concealed
___driftwood	___hammock
___lamented	___sea urchins
___sternly	___tweezers

1. For many people, the perfect vacation is to lie in a hanging mat and gaze out at the ocean.

____

2. Many fascinating sea creatures are hidden during low tide.

____

3. Tiny sea animals crawl out from holes in the rocks to eat seaweed from tide pools.

____

4. Crabs use their claws like pincers to pull food from the cracks in the rocks.

____

5. Scientists strongly warn us about the danger of destroying the ocean habitat.

____

6. Environmentalists have spoken sadly about how people pollute the ocean.

____

7. Corals live near the ocean's surface and eat very small organisms that feed off of the sunlight.

____

8. After a storm, you can often find pieces of floating wood adrift in the ocean.

____

Directions Write a sentence about *Life in the Sea* using two of the vocabulary words.

____

____

A Spy in Disguise

SEQUENCE
INFERRING

SUMMARY Students read about how Sarah Emma Edmonds succeeded in disguising her identity in order to spy for the Union Army during the Civil War.

LESSON VOCABULARY

canteen	Confederacy
glory	quarrel
rebellion	stallion
Union	

INTRODUCE THE BOOK

INTRODUCE THE TITLE AND AUTHOR Discuss the title and author of *A Spy in Disguise*. Based on the title and the illustration on the cover, ask students to describe what they think this book will be about. Ask students how they think the woman shown on the cover might disguise her identity.

BUILD BACKGROUND Discuss the Civil War with students. Have students share any background knowledge about how spies are used in wartime.

PREVIEW/USE TEXT FEATURES After students have previewed the book, discuss what they think the story is about. Have them preview the captions that accompany the illustrations and photographs and discuss ways that a woman might disguise her identity to spy on the enemy.

READ THE BOOK

SET PURPOSE Have students set a purpose for reading *A Spy in Disguise*. Ask them to think about the risks that a spy might undertake and possible rewards.

STRATEGY SUPPORT: INFERRING Tell students that readers combine the information they already know with clues from the text to understand something that is not directly stated. Ask: What clues does the author give that help readers understand why Emma Edmonds became a spy?

COMPREHENSION QUESTIONS

PAGE 3 In what ways was life not easy for Emma Edmonds when she was young? *(She worked hard on the family farm; her father quarreled often with his children and tried to force Emma to marry someone she did not know.)*

PAGES 5–6 What different jobs did Emma do in the army? *(nurse, mail carrier, spy)*

PAGES 8–9 How was Emma able to provide detailed information about Confederate plans to General McClellan? *(She listened carefully to conversations around her; she made notes and a diagram and hid these documents in her shoe. She left the camp while she was on guard duty.)*

PAGES 10–15 What do Emma's experiences of escaping from Confederate soldiers reveal about her character? *(Possible response: She was brave, daring, and clever.)*

PAGES 18-19 Why did Emma stop her spying activities? *(When she got sick and left the army, Frank Thompson was reported as a deserter. Emma was afraid she would be arrested if she disguised herself as Frank Thompson once again.)*

REVISIT THE BOOK

READER RESPONSE

1. 2, 5, 1, 3, and 4
2. Possible response: Emma Edmonds was adventurous, brave, and clever. She found creative ways to obtain important information. She risked her life again and again to provide information to help the Union army. This helps readers understand the biography as a portrait of a patriot.
3. Possible responses: *rebellion* (negative): Southern states rebelled because they did not want slavery to end; *quarrel* (negative): Many disputes can be resolved by discussion or new laws instead of by quarreling or going to war; *union* (positive): Soldiers in the union army were fighting to help others become free.
4. Responses will vary, but should identify an actual episode from Emma Edmonds' life with details that show why the adventure is interesting.

EXTEND UNDERSTANDING Discuss roles of women during the Civil War era. Explain to students that, other than working as a nurse in certain settings, there were few ways for women to get involved in supporting a cause they believed in.

RESPONSE OPTIONS

WRITING Have students write a diary entry from the point of view of Emma Edmonds during a dramatic event described in *A Spy in Disguise.*

SOCIAL STUDIES CONNECTION

Time For SOCIAL STUDIES

Provide a blank map of the eastern United States. Have students locate and label the places Emma Edmonds traveled and trace the route she followed on the map.

Skill Work

TEACH/REVIEW VOCABULARY

Write the vocabulary words on cards. Have students work in groups of four to play Password, using one-word clues to elicit one of the words from a partner. Pairs can take turns until they have completed the list. You might have them time each other to see which pair can complete the task first.

ELL Many of the vocabulary words are abstract nouns whose meanings may be difficult for students to grasp. Have students check the definitions in a dictionary and record each meaning in their own words.

TARGET SKILL AND STRATEGY

SEQUENCE Explain that biographies often follow key events in the life of the subject in the order they occurred. Explain that writers of biographies may build on events to show how different experiences help shape the person's actions in the future. Discuss how Emma Edmonds early experiences shaped her decision to become a spy.

INFERRING Remind students that when they make an inference they use what they already know to make sense of information that is not directly stated. Ask students what inferences they can make about Emma Edmonds' character.

ADDITIONAL SKILL INSTRUCTION

GENERALIZE Remind students that a generalization is a broad rule or general statement that applies to many examples. Ask students to form a generalization about why Emma Edmonds was able to spy by disguising herself as a woman or as an African American. *(Possible response: Women and African Americans were not viewed as capable or independent as white men, so people did not expect that they would be spies.)*

Name ______________________________

Sequence

- **Sequence** tells the order in which things happen.

Directions Read the following events from *A Spy in Disguise*. Write them in the correct order on the lines below.

- Emma received retirement pay for being a war veteran.
- Charles Mayberry was arrested with southern spies.
- Disguised as an Irish woman, Emma cared for a dying Confederate soldier.
- Disguised as an African-American washerwoman, Emma passed information from a Confederate officer on to Union officers.
- Emma wrote a book about her adventures.
- Emma disguised herself as a male African American slave to spy on the Confederate army.
- Emma disguised herself as Frank Thompson and worked as an army nurse.
- Emma became ill, and Frank Thompson was listed as a deserter from the army.

1. ______________________________

2. ______________________________

3. ______________________________

4. ______________________________

5. ______________________________

6. ______________________________

7. ______________________________

8. ______________________________

Name____________________________________

Vocabulary

Directions Use the vocabulary words to complete the crossword puzzle.

Check the Words You Know

___canteen	___Confederacy	___glory
___quarrel	___rebellion	___stallion
___Union		

ACROSS

1. argue
4. group of Southern states that fought in the Civil War
6. adult male horse

DOWN

2. group of Northern states that fought in the Civil War
3. armed fight against the government
4. container for drinking water
5. great fame or honor

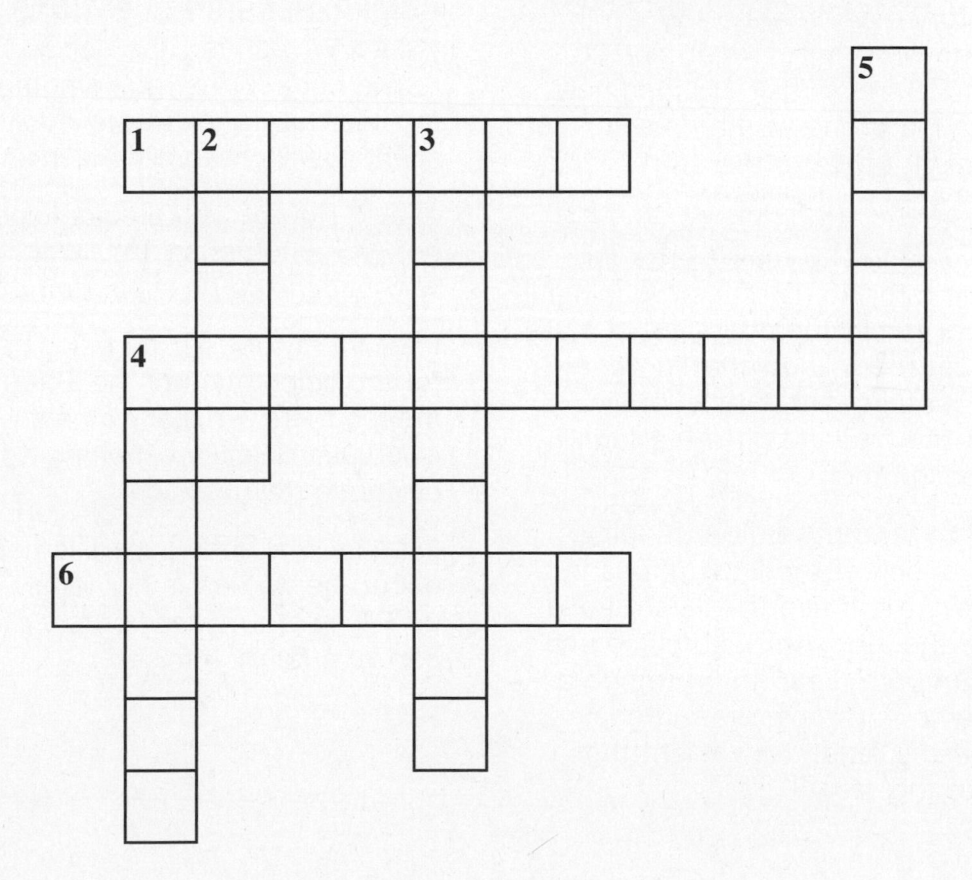

7. Use three vocabulary words to write sentences about the Civil War.

____

____

Abuela's Gift

COMPARE AND CONTRAST
STORY STRUCTURE

SUMMARY In this story, a young girl experiences the joy of both giving and receiving family-oriented gifts.

LESSON VOCABULARY

astonished	behavior
benefactor	distribution
gratitude	procession
recommend	sacred
traditions	

INTRODUCE THE BOOK

INTRODUCE THE TITLE AND AUTHOR Discuss with students the title and the author of *Abuela's Gift.* Based on the title, ask students what they think the story may be about. When students hear the word "gift," what kind of images come into their minds? Discuss how the cover illustration of the woman holding out a large pastry might relate to the story.

BUILD BACKGROUND Ask students if they have ever made, or would like to make, gifts for members of their families. Discuss meaningful types of gifts that family members could make for each other. Let them know that in *Abuela's Gift* they will be learning about how family traditions affect the types of gifts the family members give each other.

PREVIEW/USE ILLUSTRATIONS Before reading, invite students to look at the illustrations in *Abuela's Gift*. Have them use the illustrations to predict where the story will take place and who the characters are. Lead them to see a predominant theme in the pictures. (People are eating or making food.) How might those pictures relate to the story?

READ THE BOOK

SET PURPOSE Have students set a purpose for reading *Abuela's Gift*. As they read, suggest they think about the kinds of gifts members of their family give each other. Encourage them to compare their own families' gifts to the gifts in the story.

STRATEGY SUPPORT: STORY STRUCTURE Remind students that *story structure* is the way an author organizes information in a fictional book. As students read, encourage them to keep track of what happens in the beginning, middle, and end of the story.

COMPREHENSION QUESTIONS

PAGE 5 Why does Lupe decide to make a recipe book for her grandmother? *(She wants to show how thankful she is for the good times spent cooking with her grandmother.)*

PAGE 7 How do you predict Lupe will react to her grandmother's gifts? Why? *(Answers will vary but should be supported by text.)*

PAGE 9 Why does Lupe enjoy being in Mexico for the celebration of the Three Kings? *(In Mexico there are many others who share the celebration. Back in Phoenix, not many others celebrate that tradition.)*

PAGE 16 Why does Lupe like hearing stories about the women in her family making Rosca de Reyes? *(It makes her feel like an important part of a family tradition.)*

REVISIT THE BOOK

READER RESPONSE

1. Possible responses: Abuela's: all sorts of family information; Lupe's: recipes; Both: show family traditions.
2. Middle: The beginning of the book talks about family traditions and the Christmas gift Lupe wanted to make for Abuela.
3. Possible responses: *benefit, beneficial, benevolent; bene-* means "good."
4. Answers will vary.

EXTEND UNDERSTANDING Review that setting is where and when a story takes place. Ask students where most of this story takes place. *(Mexico)* Ask: How does the Mexican setting affect Lupe's Christmas experience? *(Possible response: It makes the experience special because she gets to speak Spanish, see the Three Kings Procession, spend time with family, and experience different kinds of foods.)*

RESPONSE OPTIONS

WRITING Have students think of favorite foods that their family eats. Invite them to make a list of the dishes they would like to learn how to cook. Ask them whether certain dishes are special within their familes; if so, suggest they write a paragraph describing why.

ELL Have students complete the writing activity above. Ask them to describe or draw the foods so that you can help them translate the ingredients of the foods into English.

SOCIAL STUDIES CONNECTION

Time For SOCIAL STUDIES

Review with students that celebrating the Three Kings is an important tradition in Lupe's family. Ask students to research and report on an important tradition that their own families celebrate.

Skill Work

TEACH/REVIEW VOCABULARY

Challenge students to use vocabulary words in sentences that relate to food. Example: *Since I knew Sally hated to cook, I was astonished at how delicious her soup was.*

TARGET SKILL AND STRATEGY

COMPARE AND CONTRAST Review with students that to *compare and contrast*, means to look at how things are alike and how they are different. As students read, invite them to take notes on how Lupe's and her grandmother's gifts are similar and how they are different.

STORY STRUCTURE Review with students that *story structure* is the way a fictional story is organized. All stories have events that happen in the beginning, middle, and end. Each event leads to the next event. After students finish *Abuela's Gift*, ask them to summarize what happened at each part of the story.

ADDITIONAL SKILL INSTRUCTION

THEME Review that the *theme* is the "big idea" of a story. It is the underlying meaning that the reader determines from the story's events and characters. Sometimes the author states what the theme is, but usually the reader has to use clues from the story to piece the theme together. Let students know that a story can have more than one theme. As students read *Abuela's Gift,* suggest they use the illustrations as well as the words to help them figure out what the theme or themes might be. Afterwards, discuss the theme or themes and what information the students used to determine them.

Name ______________________________

Compare and Contrast

- To **compare** is to tell how two or more things are alike or different.
- To **contrast** is to tell only how two or more things are different.

Directions Use *Abuela's Gift* to help you answer the following questions.

1. Contrast the language Lupe speaks in America with the one she speaks in Mexico.

____

____

2. Why does Lupe feel sad when she thinks about the Three Kings and her friends at home?

____

____

3. Lupe's mother tells Lupe that her mother taught her to make Rosca de Reyes. How is that different from Lupe's experience?

____

____

____

4. What are some things that are typical of the Christmas celebrations at Abuela's house?

____

____

____

5. Did using the reading skill of compare and contrast help you to understand this story better? Why or why not?

____

____

____

Name ________________________________

Vocabulary

Directions In each of the following sentences, the vocabulary words are italicized. Underline the sentences in which the vocabulary words are used correctly. Do nothing with the sentences in which the vocabulary words are used incorrectly.

Check the Words You Know

___astonished	___behavior	___benefactor
___distribution	___gratitude	___procession
___recommend	___sacred	___traditions

1. Abuela's ability to bake a great pastry is *astonished.*
2. Lupe wanted to help, so she was on her best *behavior.*
3. Helping each other cook was very *benefactor* for the family.
4. The pieces of pastry were *distribution* equally among the people at the table.
5. Lupe was filled with *gratitude* at the chance to be part of a family tradition.
6. They watched the *procession* of the Three Kings wind through the streets.
7. The *recommend* is to use three cups of flour in the recipe.
8. The recipes were *sacred* to Lupe's family.
9. *Traditions*, the Lupe's family eats a special pastry to celebrate Christmas.

Directions Select three vocabulary words and use each in a sentence.

10. ____

____

11. ____

____

12. ____

____

Helping Others

AUTHOR'S PURPOSE
MONITOR AND CLARIFY

SUMMARY Students read about some of the ways that people help others in need around the world.

LESSON VOCABULARY

bandana	bracelet
hogan	jostled
mesa	Navajo
turquoise	

INTRODUCE THE BOOK

INTRODUCE THE TITLE AND AUTHOR Discuss the title and author of *Helping Others*. Based on the title and the cover photograph, ask students to discuss what they think this book might be about. Ask students to suggest some ways the man pictured on the cover may help others.

BUILD BACKGROUND Discuss what students know about ways of helping others in need. Be sure they understand that assistance can come in many forms, including money, goods and services, as well as creative ideas for getting other people involved.

ELL Provide a web for students. In the center of the web, write *helping others*. Then have students add examples of ways that people help others. Also encourage students to add simple illustrations and words in their home language to complete the chart as they read the selection.

PREVIEW/USE TEXT FEATURES After students have previewed the book, discuss the introductory text box, captions, and photos that accompany each profile. Point out that these text features provide a quick summary of important ideas and details in the book.

READ THE BOOK

SET PURPOSE Have students set a purpose for reading *Helping Others*. You might suggest that they think about which of the individuals' profile is most surprising or most inspiring.

STRATEGY SUPPORT: MONITOR AND CLARIFY Tell students that good readers ask themselves questions to make sure their reading makes sense. Model questions to ask while reading: Does this make sense? What does this mean? What can I do to better understand this part?

COMPREHENSION QUESTIONS

PAGES 3–6 How was Talia able to make a difference in the lives of so many other people? *(Talia not only founded an organization to help people who had lost much to Hurricane Katrina, but she also set up an organization to support other children in different projects around the world.)*

PAGES 10–12 Why do people like Viola believe it is so important to focus on the education of girls? *(Educated girls improve the lives of other family members; the entire family's health improves as a result.)*

PAGES 13–18 In what ways is the work that Phymean and Kathy do similar? How is it different? *(Both women help poor families. Kathy makes sure that Navajo special education students receive gifts and necessities at holiday times. Phymean ensures that poor children in Cambodia receive an education.)*

PAGES 19–18 How does Scott's work probably improve the lives of others and create opportunities? *(Possible response: By making sure people have clean water, Scott helps them to be healthier. Healthy people are better able to complete school and contribute to their family and society.)*

REVISIT THE BOOK

READER RESPONSE

1. Possible response: to inform readers about people who help others; to inspire readers to help others
2. Possible response: reread, looked at photographs and read the captions; reviewed the text boxes to understand the main ideas
3. Responses will vary, but should include four vocabulary words in context to describe a section of the book.
4. Responses will vary, but should the name of someone the student helped, a description of the type of assistance, and a sentence describing how the students felt about helping.

EXTEND UNDERSTANDING Explain to students that profiles are brief biographies of individuals written for a particular purpose. The writer may choose to show the person profiled as a role model. Ask students to share examples of other profiles they have read and to discuss the author's likely reasons for writing these profiles.

RESPONSE OPTIONS

WRITING Have students work in groups to make up an organization that helps others in need. They can then create a flyer or web page that would tell others about their organization.

MUSIC CONNECTION

Have students create a rap or song in which they detail ways of helping others. They can work with small groups to prepare, practice and present their work to the class.

Skill Work

TEACH/REVIEW VOCABULARY

Have students create a picture dictionary entry for each vocabulary word, along with a written word meaning.

TARGET SKILL AND STRATEGY

AUTHOR'S PURPOSE Remind students that four common purposes authors have in writing are to persuade, to inform, to entertain, and to express their thoughts and feelings about a topic. Remind them also that writers may have more than one purpose for writing a single piece of text. Ask students what main purpose or purposes they think the author had in writing *Helping Others*.

MONITOR AND CLARIFY Remind students that when they *monitor and clarify,* they ask themselves questions to make sure they understand their reading. If they do not understand something, they take steps to better understand the text. Ask students to discuss parts of the text they did not understand at first and what questions they asked themselves to clarify the meaning.

ADDITIONAL SKILL INSTRUCTION

COMPARE AND CONTRAST Remind students that when they *compare* they examine how two things are alike and when they *contrast* they examine how two things are different. Ask students to choose two of the individuals profiled in *Helping Others* and to compare and contrast the people and their work.

Name ______________________________

Author's Purpose

- An **author's purpose** is the reason an author writes. Common purposes authors may have include writing to inform, to entertain, to persuade, and to express a point of view.

Directions Answer the questions below using the story *Helping Others.*

1. What do you think is the author's main purpose in writing *Helping Others*? Give two details from the selection that support this purpose.

____

____

____

2. Why do you think the author added the section entitled "How Can You Help?"

____

____

____

3. The author ends the introduction with the following statement: "Perhaps these stories will inspire you to make a difference too." Which purpose you listed in Question 1 or 2 does this sentence support?

____

____

____

4. For what purpose do you think the author included the photographs in this book?

____

____

____

Name ______________________________

Vocabulary

Directions Use vocabulary words to complete the crossword puzzle.

Check the Words You Know

___bandana ___bracelet ___hogan
___jostled ___mesa ___Navajo
___turquoise

ACROSS

1. shoved or pushed
2. jewelry worn on the wrist
3. Native American living in Southwest US
4. Navajo dwelling

DOWN

5. greenish-blue mineral
6. raised plateau with flat top and steep walls
7. bright cloth worn around the head or neck

Paul Revere and the American Revolutionary War 5.2.5

AUTHOR'S PURPOSE
BACKGROUND KNOWLEDGE

SUMMARY The author describes the activities of Paul Revere before the early battles of the American Revolution. In addition, the author sets the stage for the conflict behind the American Revolution by reviewing the disagreements between the American colonists and the British.

LESSON VOCABULARY

fate	fearless
glimmer	lingers
magnified	somber
steed	

INTRODUCE THE BOOK

INTRODUCE THE TITLE AND AUTHOR Discuss with students the title and the author of *Paul Revere and the American Revolutionary War.* Ask students to think about the title and what the book will be about. Discuss why the author may have chosen to focus on the activities of Paul Revere. Ask: What do you know about Paul Revere, and what would you like to know about him?

BUILD BACKGROUND Discuss with students what they know about dealing with a situation in which someone's rights are not respected. Ask: What are some of the basic American freedoms? What action would you take to protect your freedoms if someone tried to take them away?

PREVIEW/USE ILLUSTRATIONS Encourage students to look at the illustrations in the book. Ask them to choose one and explain what it seems to tell about the book. Suggest that they check after their reading to see if their prediction was correct. Ask students to study the image in the stamp place on page 7. Discuss what it might mean to the story of the American Revolution.

READ THE BOOK

SET PURPOSE Encourage students to set a purpose for their reading that includes realizing how sequence and cause and effect can help their understanding of historical material. Suggest that they list events and analyze them for sequence. Students can also list events that were causes, events that were effects, and events that served both purposes.

STRATEGY SUPPORT: BACKGROUND KNOWLEDGE To tap into students' background knowledge, encourage them to share what they already know about the American Revolution. As students preview the book, ask: Do any of these pictures or photographs remind you of something you have encountered before?

COMPREHENSION QUESTIONS

PAGE 4 What was the purpose of a liberty tree? *(Colonists posted complaints and gathered there to discuss their problems with the British.)*

PAGES 5–6 What event came before the American Revolution that caused the British to go deeply into debt? *(The French and Indian War)*

PAGE 7 Why did the colonists oppose taxation so fiercely? *(They had no voice in the British government.)*

PAGES 11–12 How did a misunderstanding about the Boston Massacre contribute to tensions between Americans and the British? *(Although it is possible that the massacre was a mistake, Paul Revere publicized it as an intentional act on the part of the British, and the Americans grew angry.)*

REVISIT THE BOOK

READER RESPONSE

1. The French and Indian War caused the British government to be deeply in debt. The government decided to tax the colonists to pay this debt.
2. Responses will vary about what students knew before reading the book and what they learned after reading the book.
   Possible responses for the time line:
   1764 Sugar Act
   1765 Stamp Act
   1770 Boston Massacre
   1773 Tea Act
   1774 First Continental Congress
3. Possible response: In the *glimmer* of the candle, I saw a *steed* go by my window. He had a *somber* tread, as though he knew his master's *fate.* But as the danger *magnified,* his master became even more *fearless,* and the two easily jumped over the high fence. The memory of their brave leap still *lingers* in my mind.
4. Possible response: White pants were hard to keep clean.

EXTEND UNDERSTANDING Encourage students to look at the title page and the illustrations on pages 10 and 17. Discuss some of the differences between the American and British soldiers. Ask: How might these differences have affected the fighting ability of the two groups of soldiers?

RESPONSE OPTIONS

WRITING Ask students to write a few paragraphs explaining why they would nominate Paul Revere as a great American hero. Encourage them to include details from the book to support their nomination.

SOCIAL STUDIES CONNECTION

Time For SOCIAL STUDIES

Encourage students to find out information about the Boston Tea Party that describes the drama of the event. Suggest that they check the Internet or the library to see whether any short stories, poems, or plays have been written about it.

Skill Work

TEACH/REVIEW VOCABULARY

Ask students to identify the nouns among the vocabulary words. *(fate, steed,* and *glimmer)* Discuss the other parts of speech that are used (adjectives and verbs) and identify them.

ELL Remind students that a noun is the name of a person, place, or thing. Point to objects around the classroom and identify them as nouns. Ask students to name additional nouns. Remind them of the nouns on the vocabulary list.

Explain the meaning of a verb. Act out *writing* on the board, and explain that the word *writing* is a verb. Remind students of the verb on the vocabulary list. Explain the meaning of an adjective. Point to someone's colored shirt and explain that the color is an adjective. Remind students of the adjectives on the vocabulary list.

TARGET SKILL AND STRATEGY

AUTHOR'S PURPOSE Remind students that an author may write for different purposes—to inform, to persuade, to entertain, or to express feelings. Based on their previews, ask students what they think the author's purpose was for writing *Paul Revere and the American Revolutionary War.*

BACKGROUND KNOWLEDGE Remind students that *background knowledge* is what readers already know about a given topic from reading or personal experience. Have students share how their background knowledge helped them as they read the book.

ADDITIONAL SKILL INSTRUCTION

CAUSE AND EFFECT Remind students that an *effect* is an event that happens, and a *cause* is why an event happens. Explain that there can be many causes that lead to one effect, as in the American Revolution. Discuss some of the possible causes. Encourage students to think about the American Revolution. Even though it was an effect, it also was a cause, because it led to a state of independence for the colonists—another *effect.*

Name ______________________________

Author's Purpose

- An **author's purpose** is the reason an author writes something. Some purposes an author may have are to persuade, to inform, to entertain, and to express a mood or feeling.
- An author may have more than one purpose for writing a particular selection.

Directions Refer to the selection to answer the questions below.

1. What do you think is the author's purpose for writing *Paul Revere and the American Revolutionary War*?

____

____

____

2. Why do you think the author includes pictures and labels of a British soldier and a colonial militiaman?

____

____

____

3. Why do you think the author uses headings within the story? Choose one heading and write two interesting facts from the story about it.

____

____

____

4. Why do you think the author ends the selection the way she does?

____

____

____

Name____

Vocabulary

Directions Draw a line from each word to its synonym.

Check the Words You Know			
___fate	___fearless	___glimmer	___lingers
___magnified	___somber	___steed	

1. fate	increased
2. fearless	unafraid
3. glimmer	uncontrolled event
4. lingers	horse
5. magnified	faint light
6. somber	stays
7. steed	solemn

Directions Write a paragraph about the beginning of the American Revolution. Use as many vocabulary words as you can.

____

____

____

____

____

____

____

____

____

____

____

____

The Search for a Perpetual Motion Machine

5.3.1

SEQUENCE OF EVENTS
SUMMARIZE

SUMMARY This nonfiction selection traces the history of attempts to build a machine that moves on its own without outside help and without stopping. The quest begins in the twelfth century and continues to the present day. This selection explores whether past attempts to build this type of machine have been successful and questions whether such a machine can truly be constructed.

LESSON VOCABULARY

applauds	browsing
fabulous	inspecting
project	

INTRODUCE THE BOOK

INTRODUCE THE TITLE AND AUTHOR Discuss with students the title and the author of *The Search for a Perpetual Motion Machine*. Ask students to think about the title and what the book will be about. Discuss with students the meanings of the words *quest* and *perpetual*.

BUILD BACKGROUND Elicit from students what they have previously learned about the different types of energy, such as light, heat, and electricity. Explain that energy is defined as the ability to do work and that a scientific law states that it cannot be created or destroyed.

ELL Ask students if they know the words for *energy, light, heat,* and *electricity* in another language. Encourage them to share what they know about these topics.

PREVIEW/USE TEXT FEATURES Have students read the chapter headings and look through the photographs and illustrations in the book. Invite them to read the captions that accompany the pictures and ask: How do the captions help you better understand what you see in the pictures?

READ THE BOOK

SET PURPOSE Have students set a purpose for their reading and keep track of the most important information related to that purpose. Suggest that a good way to keep track of information is to take notes as you read.

STRATEGY SUPPORT: SUMMARIZE As students read, summarizing helps them understand the important parts of the book. Have students write short summaries of each section based on their understanding of each section's main idea. Encourage them to include a few supporting details in each summary to support the main idea.

COMPREHENSION QUESTIONS

PAGE 6 What is a perpetual motion machine? *(a machine that moves itself, without anything to push or drive it; once started, it keeps moving without outside help)*

PAGE 9 Why did the author use a question as the title of this chapter? *(because the author doesn't know the answer to the question; she uses the chapter to explore the question)*

PAGE 19 What are some reasons people believe Johann Bessler did not invent a perpetual motion machine? *(He kept parts of his machine covered; he locked it away in a closed room; when he found out a scientist had inspected his machine, he destroyed it.)*

PAGE 23 What is the author's viewpoint regarding the possibility of a perpetual motion machine being invented? What makes you think so? *(She thinks it is possible; she says that there is "much we don't know about our world," and that "every day brings new ideas.")*

REVISIT THE BOOK

READER RESPONSE

1. Descriptions will vary, but students should list Bhaskara, Leonardo da Vinci, John Wilkins, and Johann Bessler.
2. Responses will vary.
3. Charts will vary. Possible antonyms: *terrible, horrible, awful*. Possible synonyms: *great, wonderful, terrific*.
4. Conclusions will vary but should include elaborative support, either from the book or from students' reading of the text.

EXTEND UNDERSTANDING Invite students to look at the pictures on pages 5 and 11. Have them read the accompanying captions and ask them to discuss the similarities and differences between the two machines.

RESPONSE OPTIONS

WRITING Invite students to write a few paragraphs describing an invention that would make the world a better place in which to live. What would the invention do? How would it work? What materials would they need for the invention?

WORD WORK Have students review the word *inventor* on page 17. Discuss how the verb *invent* becomes a noun describing a person who invents by adding *-or* to the end. Repeat this approach with the word *actor*.

SCIENCE CONNECTION

TIME FOR Science

Have students choose one of the inventors discussed in the book, research that inventor's life, and share their findings with the class. Suggest they use the Internet or the library to do their research.

Skill Work

TEACH/REVIEW VOCABULARY

After you discuss the meanings of the vocabulary words, have students brainstorm to come up with as many synonyms and antonyms as they can for each word.

TARGET SKILL AND STRATEGY

SEQUENCE OF EVENTS Remind students that when we read, we put information in *sequence* to help us understand it. Discuss some of the events in this book that could be put in sequence.

SUMMARIZE Remind students that to *summarize* is to boil down a selection to its most important points. Have students use the sequence of events from above to write a short summary of the story.

ADDITIONAL SKILL INSTRUCTION

DRAW CONCLUSIONS Remind students that when we *draw conclusions*, we arrive at ideas based on facts or information we have read. Suggest that they read the second paragraph on page 13. Ask: What conclusions can you draw about John Wilkins?

Name ____________________

Sequence of Events

- The **sequence of events** refers to the order of events in both fiction and nonfiction.
- Sequence can also refer to steps in a process.

Directions Use the selection to list the steps of John Wilkins's magnet machine. Put the steps in sequential order.

1. First,

____

____

____

2. Next,

____

____

____

3. Then,

____

____

____

4. Last,

____

____

____

Name____

Vocabulary

Directions Write a sentence using each of the vocabulary words. Try to make the sentences relate to a scientific invention.

Check the Words You Know

___applauds ___browsing ___fabulous ___inspecting ___project

1. ____
____

2. ____
____

3. ____
____

4. ____
____

5. ____
____

Directions Draw a line from the vocabulary word to its definition.

6. applauds	**a.** wonderful; exciting
7. browsing	**b.** looking over carefully; examining
8. fabulous	**c.** shows approval by clapping the hands
9. inspecting	**d.** a plan; scheme; effort; undertaking
10. project	**e.** looking here and there

The Italian Renaissance and Its Artists

5.3.2

MAIN IDEA AND DETAILS
VISUALIZE

SUMMARY Michelangelo, Raphael, da Vinci, and Donatello had a major influence on the style of art in the Italian Renaissance period. They focused their art on humanism, depicting emotions and scenes from everyday life.

LESSON VOCABULARY

achieved	architect
bronze	cannon
depressed	fashioned
midst	philosopher
rival	

INTRODUCE THE BOOK

INTRODUCE THE TITLE AND AUTHOR Discuss with students the title and the author of *The Italian Renaissance and Its Artists*. Based on the title, ask students what kind of information they think this book will provide. Ask them if they think the book will be fiction or nonfiction.

BUILD BACKGROUND Discuss with students what they know about types of art, such as paintings or sculptures. Have volunteers share their favorite types of art with the class.

PREVIEW/USE TEXT FEATURES As students preview the book, ask them to look at the illustrations in the book and read the captions. Draw their attention to the various types of art shown. Ask students what they think the book will teach them.

READ THE BOOK

SET PURPOSE Have students set a purpose for reading *The Italian Renaissance and Its Artists*. Encourage them to think about the important facts in the book as they read. Ask them to pay attention to the illustrations to enhance their understanding.

STRATEGY SUPPORT: VISUALIZE As students read, encourage them to use the descriptions from the text to form pictures in their minds. Explain that this will help them understand the information better. Model visualizing on page 13. Say: The text says that Michelangelo was frustrated and frequently erased his work and fired his assistants. I can see him being very angry and short with the people around him. I can imagine that he felt like this project was impossible.

COMPREHENSION QUESTIONS

PAGE 7 What is the main idea of the last paragraph? *(The focus of art changed from religion to everyday life.)*

PAGE 13 How long did it take Michelangelo to paint the Sistine Chapel? *(four years)*

PAGE 14 What generalization is made about people during the time Michelangelo lived? *(Few people lived to the age of fifty.)*

PAGE 20 Summarize the second paragraph. *(Da Vinci was one of the first artists to use oil-based paints. He also painted frescoes.)*

REVISIT THE BOOK

READER RESPONSE

1. Main idea: Michelangelo had a hard time painting the Sistine Chapel. Supporting details: He had to relearn painting; he supposedly fired his assistants; it took him four years to finish.
2. Responses will vary, but students should include a detailed description and explain how visualizing helped them better understand the book.
3. Possible responses: *repress, suppress, impress, express*
4. Possible response: *Mona Lisa,* because she has a lifelike smile

EXTEND UNDERSTANDING Ask students to look at the illustrations in the book. Ask them how the pictures help them better understand the descriptions of the art in the book.

RESPONSE OPTIONS

WRITING Have students choose one of the illustrations from the book and tell how the artwork shows humanism. Remind students that humanism shows emotions and people and things in everyday life.

ART CONNECTION

Encourage students to look at other works of art by Michelangelo or the other artists portrayed in this book. Have them find photos in a library book or on the Internet.

Skill Work

TEACH/REVIEW VOCABULARY

Review vocabulary words and their definitions with students. Divide students into small groups. Assign each group a vocabulary word and have the group come up with two sentences using the word. Ask a member from each group to write their sentences on the board.

TARGET SKILL AND STRATEGY

MAIN IDEA AND DETAILS Remind students that the *main idea* is the most important idea about a topic. As they read, have students write a short sentence that tells the main idea of each of the sections.

ELL Encourage students to use a graphic organizer to help them identify the main idea in each section of this book. Have them write down details that support the main idea.

VISUALIZE Remind students that when they *visualize*, they are able to create pictures in their mind that will help them better understand the text. Have students read page 23. Ask: What do the words and descriptions help you to visualize? *(Possible response: It helps me visualize the excitement people were feeling, being so inspired and ready to create new works.)*

ADDITIONAL SKILL INSTRUCTION

GENERALIZE Remind students that sometimes when you read, you are given ideas about several things or people, and you can make a statement about all of them together. This statement is called a *generalization*. Valid generalizations are accurate or true. As students read, have them write down generalizations about artists in the Italian Renaissance period.

Name ____

Main Idea and Details

- The **main idea** is the most important idea about a paragraph, passage, or article.
- **Supporting details** are small pieces of information that tell more about the main idea.

Directions Read the paragraph below. Then complete the graphic organizer by writing the main idea of that passage. List details that tell more about the main idea.

Artists shifted art away from its original focus on religion. Their paintings focused less on religious teachings and more on human emotions and the drama of everyday life. Historians now use the term *humanism* to describe this style of art.

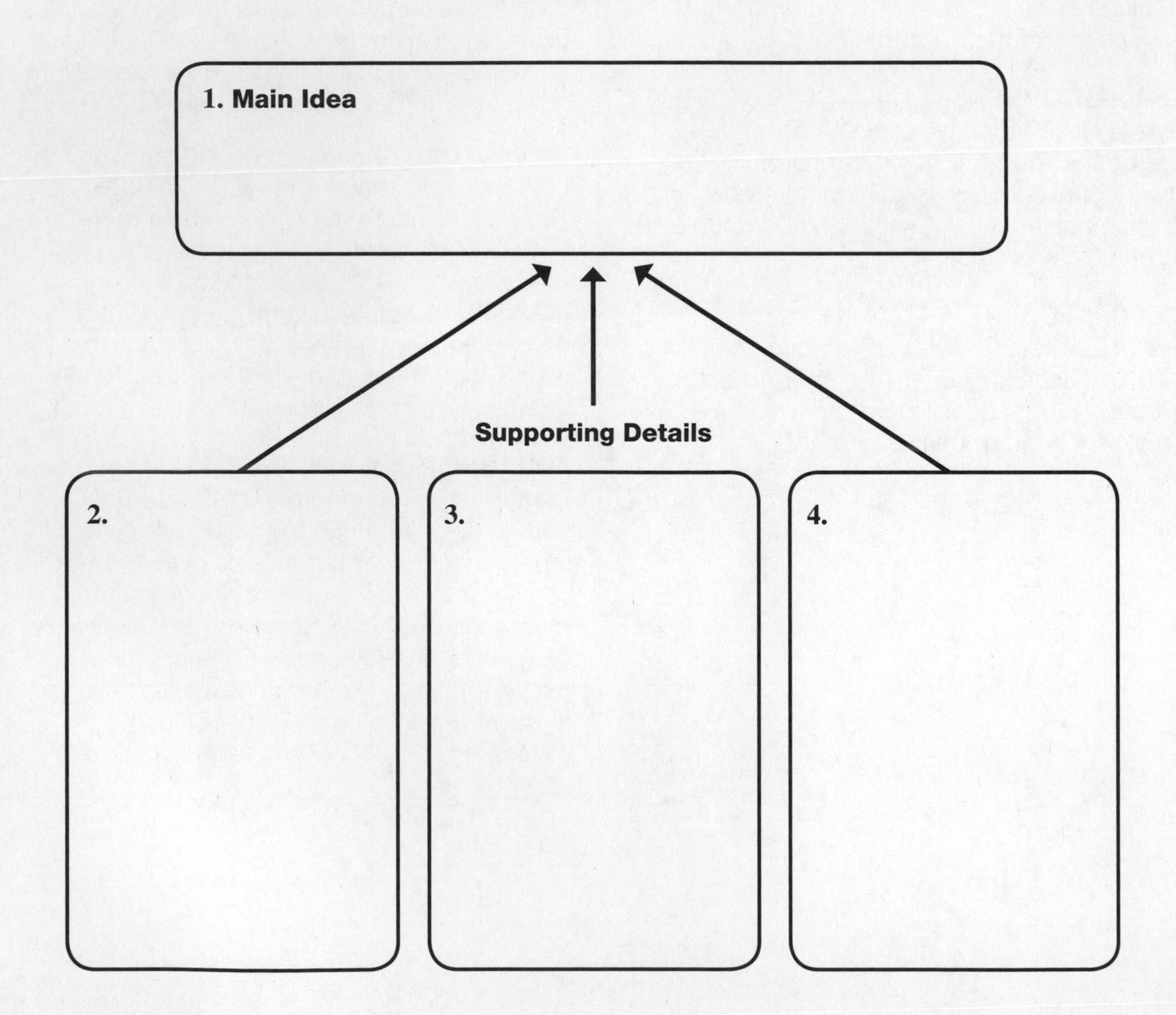

Name ____

Vocabulary

Directions Draw a line from each word to its definition.

Check the Words You Know

___achieved	___architect	___bronze
___cannon	___depressed	___fashioned
___midst	___philosopher	___rival

1. achieved	gloomy
2. architect	person who tries to understand the nature of reality
3. bronze	formed
4. cannon	accomplished
5. depressed	the middle of
6. fashioned	competitor
7. midst	person who designs buildings
8. philosopher	alloy of copper and tin
9. rival	big gun

Directions Write a sentence for each of the following words: *architect, fashioned, midst, philosopher, rival.*

10. ____

____

11. ____

____

12. ____

____

13. ____

____

14. ____

____

Searching for Dinosaurs

5.3.3

FACT AND OPINION
PREDICT

SUMMARY This book explores the careers and impact of various important paleontologists. It also explains animatronics, the technology used to build robotic models of dinosaurs.

LESSON VOCABULARY

erected	foundation	mold
occasion	proportion	tidied
workshop		

INTRODUCE THE BOOK

INTRODUCE THE TITLE AND AUTHOR Discuss with students the title and author of *Searching for Dinosaurs*. Ask students to try to identify the image in the photo *(fossil)*. Ask students to tell of any other books they've read on dinosaurs. Do they think this book will be fiction or nonfiction? Why? *(nonfiction; the label on the cover says Life Science)*

BUILD BACKGROUND If needed, define *paleontologist.* (See page 6.) Have students share any knowledge of paleontology or experience looking for fossils. Also explore knowledge and interest in robotics. Ask if anyone has seen robotic models of dinosaurs.

PREVIEW/USE TEXT FEATURES As students look through the book, draw their attention to the map on page 9. Have them point out the key and the symbol used to represent dinosaur finds. Then have students use the illustrations and headings in the book to predict what the book will be about.

READ THE BOOK

SET PURPOSE Have students set purposes for reading *Searching for Dinosaurs*. Students' own interest in fossils, dinosaurs, and robotics should help guide their purposes. Students may want to know where different fossils are found and how they serve as models for making robotic versions of dinosaurs.

STRATEGY SUPPORT: PREDICT Discuss that it is important to keep revising, or changing predictions, based on new information. Before students read the section on animatronics, have them preview the section headings and pictures. What do they think they will learn about how animatronics are made? Have students write down their answers. Then, after they read pages 16–17, they should revisit their prediction and rewrite it using new knowledge they have gained from the text. Finally, after completing the section showing all the steps in animatronics, they should go back and read their last prediction, noting what part of it was correct. Afterwards, discuss the predictions and revisions as a group.

COMPREHENSION QUESTIONS

PAGE 4 Why is Sue such a famous fossil? *(It is the largest and most complete Tyrannosaurus rex fossil ever found.)*

PAGE 13 What word in the heading makes this statement an opinion? *(amazing)*

PAGE 14 How was Joan Wiffen's educational background different from that of many other modern fossil hunters? *(She did not have a degree in paleontology.)*

PAGES 18–21 How do the pictures on these pages help you predict what you will learn about animatronics? *(Answers will vary.)*

REVISIT THE BOOK

READER RESPONSE

1. Possible response: Facts: In 1995 Sereno and Lynn led a fossil-hunting team to Africa. In 1997 David Varricchio . . . spotted a fossil claw sticking out of the desert sand. Opinions: The trip's highlight occurred when Sereno discovered a fossil skull . . . It was a great find, but even more lay in store.
2. Answers will vary.
3. It is important because everything else rests on, depends on, or is built on it.
4. Answers will vary.

EXTEND UNDERSTANDING Direct students to the chart on page 18. Elicit that it is a summary of the steps involved in making animatronics. Discuss whether or not having the chart to refer to helped students understand and organize the steps better.

ELL To check students' understanding, have them retell sections of the text in their own words. Allow them to point to illustrations to help with the retelling.

RESPONSE OPTIONS

WRITING Invite students to choose one of the fossil hunters in this book and write that person a letter. What would students like to say to him or her? What would they ask?

SCIENCE CONNECTION

TIME FOR Science

Have students further research dinosaurs and dinosaur fossils. Then invite them to use modeling clay to recreate a chosen dinosaur or dinosaur fossil. Have students label and display their creations.

Skill Work

TEACH/REVIEW VOCABULARY

Many of the words have multiple meanings. To clarify the usage of these and other vocabulary words, discuss the contextual meanings: *occasion*, page 14; *mold,* page 18; *foundation,* page 19; *proportion,* page 19; *tidied,* page 20; *workshop,* page 23; *erected,* page 23.

TARGET SKILL AND STRATEGY

FACT AND OPINION Remind students that a *statement of fact* can be proved true or false. A *statement of opinion* is someone's judgment, belief, or way of thinking. Read the last sentence on page 6. Ask: Can this statement be proved? *(No; the words* greatly *and* respected *make it an opinion.)* Then read the first sentence on the page and have students tell if it is a statement of fact or opinion. *(fact)* Tell students that as they read, they should ask themselves if the information they are learning is fact or opinion.

PREDICT Remind students that to *predict* means to tell what you think might happen next in a book, article, or story based on what has already happened and prior knowledge of the subject. Tell students to note that in *Searching for Dinosaurs*, the author uses a mix of fact and opinion. As students read, they should bear this style in mind to help them predict what facts they will learn about fossil hunters and their discoveries.

ADDITIONAL SKILL INSTRUCTION

COMPARE AND CONTRAST Remind students that to *compare* is to identify how two or more things are alike, and to *contrast* is to identify how they are different. To help students understand the differences between computer special effects and animatronics, have them construct a Venn diagram. As students read, suggest they jot down some notes comparing the two processes.

Name ____________________

Fact and Opinion

- A **statement of fact** is one that can be proved true or false.
- A **statement of opinion** is a statement of someone's judgment, belief, or way of thinking.

Directions Read each sentence below. Write whether the sentence is a statement of fact or of opinion.

1. ____________ Probably the best explanation for why people become fossil hunters is curiosity.

2. ____________ Today, the field of dinosaur paleontology is thriving, thanks to the efforts of many world-renowned scientists.

3. ____________ Since the early 1800s, scientists on several different continents have discovered more than 300 dinosaur species.

4. ____________ Paul Sereno worked hard in college and graduate school to make his dream of becoming a dinosaur paleontologist a reality.

5. ____________ *Suchomimus* was given its name because scientists believe that it ate like a crocodile.

6. ____________ Joan Wiffen worked hard to overcome the scientists' lack of faith in her abilities as a paleontologist.

7. ____________ A full-sized model can be made by hand or through such modern manufacturing techniques as CAM (Computer-Assisted Manufacturing).

8. ____________ The artists and engineers have done their best to create the best possible model for the museumgoer or moviegoer to see, hear, and enjoy.

Directions Write one statement of fact about dinosaurs. Then write one statement of opinion.

9. ____

____

10. ____

____

Name ______________________________

Vocabulary

Directions Write the word next to its definition and then use the word in a sentence.

Check the Words You Know

___erected	___foundation	___mold	___occasion
___proportion	___tidied	___workshop	

1. put in order; made neat ____________

____

____

2. particular time ____________

____

____

3. part on which other parts rest ____________

____

____

4. building or area where work is done ____________

____

____

5. a proper relation among parts ____________

____

____

6. built; set up ____________

____

____

7. a hollow form in which material is poured and shaped ____________

____

____

Blues Legends

MAIN IDEA AND DETAILS
TEXT STRUCTURE

SUMMARY This book explores the history of blues music by discussing the careers of famous musicians such as Ma Rainey, Bessie Smith, Ray Charles, and Aretha Franklin.

LESSON VOCABULARY

appreciate	barber
choir	released
religious	slavery
teenager	

INTRODUCE THE BOOK

INTRODUCE THE TITLE AND AUTHOR Discuss with students the title and the author of *Blues Legends*. Make sure students understand that the word *legends* refers to famous people. Ask students to tell you what they think the blues are. Ask students if they can think of how this book might relate to a social studies topic.

BUILD BACKGROUND Play the music of one or more of the artists mentioned in the book. Ask if students are familiar with this music. Then have students share any knowledge they might have about blues music or any of the musicians mentioned in the book.

PREVIEW/USE TEXT FEATURES Point out the Biography label on the cover and the headings throughout the book that tell whom each section will be about. Have students note that the book first gives a little background on the origin of the blues before giving the biographies of blues musicians.

READ THE BOOK

SET PURPOSE Have students set a purpose for reading *Blues Legends*. Students' interest in music and history should guide this purpose. Suggest that students think about how different musicians learn from each other and how historical events can affect musical styles.

STRATEGY SUPPORT: TEXT STRUCTURE As students read, have them pay attention to the way the text is organized. Explain that in a nonfiction text, the author can use captions and headings to draw attention to important ideas. Ask: What does the caption on page 3 draw attention to?

COMPREHENSION QUESTIONS

PAGES 8–9 Why do you think the author chose to show pictures of old phonographs? *(Responses will vary.)*

PAGE 9 What is the main idea of the first paragraph? *(Rainey's music often dealt with problems facing African Americans.)*

PAGES 10–13 Do you think a time line would be a good graphic to show the information on these pages? Why or why not? *(Possible response: Yes; it could show the order of what happened in Bessie's life.)*

PAGE 23 What are some roots of the blues? *(African culture and American slavery)*

REVISIT THE BOOK

READER RESPONSE

1. Main Idea: The Great Depression hurt Bessie Smith's career. Details: People wanted upbeat music instead of blues; people had less money to spend on concerts and records.
2. Possible response: Each of the headings told me what that section of the book would be about.
3. increase in value; possible sentence: The stock should appreciate in value once the company is sold.
4. Responses will vary.

EXTEND UNDERSTANDING Ask students to think about the photos in *Blues Legends.* Ask: What information do they give you that you could not have gotten from the text alone?

RESPONSE OPTIONS

ART Provide students with a variety of blues music to listen to. Encourage students to draw or paint pictures inspired by listening to the blues.

SOCIAL STUDIES CONNECTION

Time For SOCIAL STUDIES

Ask students to find out more about other famous blues musicians and to write a brief biography of one of them. Post the biographies on the bulletin board.

Skill Work

TEACH/REVIEW VOCABULARY

Copy the vocabulary words onto index cards. Have students randomly draw cards and use the words in sentences that relate to music. For example: My barber plays country music while cutting my hair.

ELL Help students understand that the word *released* can have more than one meaning. In this book, it means "to be published or sold." The other meaning is "set free."

TARGET SKILL AND STRATEGY

MAIN IDEA AND DETAILS Remind students that the *main idea* is the most important idea about a topic. Supporting *details* are small pieces of information that tell more about the main idea. To practice finding the main idea, read pages 6–7 aloud and have students identify the topic. (*Ma Rainey*) Then ask them to decide what important idea about the topic all the sentences in the section contribute to. (*Possible response: Ma Rainey was an important and influential blues singer.*) Tell students to use this method as they look for the main idea and supporting details in other sections of this book.

TEXT STRUCTURE Remind students that *text structure* is how information in a nonfiction text is organized. As students read, have them point out different ways the author organizes important information. Call attention to the captions and headings. Ask students how each of these help them understand the information better.

ADDITIONAL SKILL INSTRUCTION

AUTHOR'S PURPOSE Remind students that an author can have several purposes for writing—for example, to inform, to persuade, to entertain, or to express feelings. Ask: What do you think is the author's purpose for writing *Blues Legends*?

Name ______________________________

Main Idea and Details

- The **main idea** is the most important idea about a paragraph, passage, or article.
- **Supporting details** are small pieces of information that tell more about the main idea.

Directions Read the following passage. Complete the diagram by writing the main idea of the passage. Then list supporting details that tell more about the main idea.

Ray had a difficult childhood. He grew up during the worst of the Great Depression; his family had very little money. At the age of six, Ray began losing his sight and became completely blind by age seven. On top of this, Ray, like Bessie Smith, had to deal with the early deaths of his parents. Ray's father died when Ray was only ten. His mother died when he was just fifteen. Somehow, Ray found a way to overcome these hardships and developed into a great blues artist.

Main Idea

____

____

____

Supporting Details

____

____

____

____

____

____

Name ______________________________

Vocabulary

Directions Unscramble the vocabulary words and then use each one in a sentence.

Check the Words You Know

___appreciate ___barber ___choir
___released ___religious ___slavery
___teenager

1. oicrh ____________________

____

____

2. reeentga ____________________

____

____

3. abrbre ____________________

____

____

4. dreeslea ____________________

____

____

5. teappaicer ____________________

____

____

6. sigoiulre ____________________

____

____

7. vsaleyr ____________________

____

____

Computers in Filmmaking: Very Special Effects

5.3.5

GRAPHIC SOURCES
IMPORTANT IDEAS

SUMMARY Movies made today include many computerized special effects to create characters and scenes. In addition, a growing number of movies are being shot entirely with computers, creating benefits for moviegoers, but complex issues for theaters.

LESSON VOCABULARY

background	landscape
miniature	prehistoric
reassembled	

INTRODUCE THE BOOK

INTRODUCE THE TITLE AND AUTHOR Discuss with students the title and the author of *Computers in Filmmaking: Very Special Effects*. Ask students what they can tell about the book based on the cover illustration.

BUILD BACKGROUND Ask students to discuss films they've seen recently that have used computerized special effects. Ask: How did you know that parts of those films were made using computers? Students might mention *A Bug's Life, The Incredibles, Finding Nemo,* or *Toy Story*. Ask: Why do you like special effects?

PREVIEW/USE TEXT FEATURES Have students preview the text by looking at photos, captions, the chart on pages 20–21, and the subheads throughout. Remind students that text features can help organize their reading.

READ THE BOOK

SET PURPOSE Have students set a purpose for reading *Computers in Filmmaking: Very Special Effects*. Some students may be curious about how computerized characters are created. Others may have an interest in becoming computer animators or in using home digital video cameras to make their own movies.

STRATEGY SUPPORT: IMPORTANT IDEAS Remind students that *important ideas* tell more about the main topic of the story. Important ideas are supported by details. As students read, have them list important ideas from the story and the details that support these ideas.

COMPREHENSION QUESTIONS

PAGES 4–5 How has computerized filmmaking helped directors? *(They can create vibrant sets on a computer rather than on a big stage; they can cover up background objects or add objects.)*

PAGE 6 What did early special effects use? *(hand-drawn animation, clay models or puppets)*

PAGE 11 How does the graphic source on page 11 help explain rotoscoping? *(It shows how the frames of film are outlined and then blanked out.)*

PAGE 14 What happens during compositing? *(Layers of computer graphic work are placed one atop the next; then the digital file is turned to film.)*

PAGE 19 How are computer-based digital movies edited? *(Computer code can simply be rearranged—like cutting and pasting text.)*

PAGE 23 Why is the movie industry worried about computerized movies? *(Since digital movies can be downloaded, moviegoers might go to theaters less.)*

REVISIT THE BOOK

READER RESPONSE

1. Responses will vary but should cite specific elements of specific images.
2. Responses will vary.
3. Possible response: Miniature sets are much cheaper and easier to build than complex, full-sized sets as backgrounds for the action.
4. Responses will vary.

EXTEND UNDERSTANDING Focus students on pages 4–5, 6–7, and 18–19. Each pair of illustrations displays old and new techniques for making movies. For each pair, ask students: How do these two pictures show how moviemaking has changed? Which do you like better? Why?

ELL Encourage students to make a graphic organizer that outlines the steps to create computer-animated characters. First, they should write the three steps of the *preproduction process* as on page 8. Next, write the steps of the *postproduction process*, as on pages 9–15.

RESPONSE OPTIONS

WRITING Have each student write a few paragraphs about a computer-animated character he or she would like to create. Remind students to make their descriptions as vivid as possible so they can be turned over to a Hollywood animator. (Have students include sketches of their characters.)

WORD WORK The vocabulary for this text includes two compound words (*background* and *landscape*). Remind students that a compound word is a single word made of two smaller words. Ask each student to come up with five additional compound words, define them, and share several with the group.

SOCIAL STUDIES CONNECTION

Time For SOCIAL STUDIES

Have students use the Internet to research movie studios that are using computer animation, such as Pixar, which has a Web site with a detailed time line that explains the company's humble beginnings and traces its development. Have students prepare short reports on their findings.

Skill Work

TEACH/REVIEW VOCABULARY

Have students define vocabulary words they know and discuss words they don't. Suggest that students create a list of other words they would like to learn, such as *pixel, preproduction, postproduction,* and *rotoscoping*.

TARGET SKILL AND STRATEGY

GRAPHIC SOURCES Remind students that a *graphic source* is a way of showing information visually. Graphics used in this text include photos with captions and a chart on pages 20–21. Encourage students to note particular graphics that make the text easier to understand. This will be useful when studying *rotoscoping* on pages 10–11.

IMPORTANT IDEAS Tell students that *important ideas* are the major parts of a story. Explain that each important idea is supported by details. As students read each section, ask: What is an important idea from this section? What details support it?

ADDITIONAL SKILL INSTRUCTION

PRIOR KNOWLEDGE Help students comprehend the text better by activating their prior knowledge. Ask: Can you think of other books or experiences that helped you better understand this text? How did these other sources help you better understand the text?

Name ____________________

Graphic Sources

- **Graphic sources** include items such as advertisements, charts, diagrams, graphs, maps, menus, photographs, recipes, and timetables.
- Use graphic sources to help you understand text and to draw conclusions as you read.

Directions Use the graphic source on pages 20–21 of *Computers in Filmmaking: Very Special Effects* to answer the questions below.

1. What type of graphic source is shown on these pages?

____

2. Give one *pro* of computer-based movies that is related to their cost.

____

____

3. What is one *con* of computer-based movies that relates to computer memory?

____

____

4. Why might movie-theater owners resist converting to computer-based films?

____

____

5. Why might moviemakers prefer computer-based movies?

____

____

6. What are some words that mean the same as *con* as it is used in this graphic source?

____

7. What are some words that mean the same as *pro* as it is used in this graphic source?

____

8. If you were a moviegoer, would you be in favor of or opposed to computer-based movies? Explain your reasoning.

____

____

____

Name ___________________________

Vocabulary

Directions Choose the word from the box that best matches each definition. Write the word on the line.

Check the Words You Know

___ background ___ landscape ___ miniature
___ prehistoric ___ reassembled

1. ________________ from a time before people began writing and keeping records
2. ________________ in a movie, the images that show up behind the actors and other objects in the foreground
3. ________________ something that has been done or made on a very small scale
4. ________________ brought things back together again
5. ________________ thc look and quality of the land when viewed from far away

Directions Complete each sentence using a word from the box above.

6. After the film is scanned into the computer, it is ________________ in a digital format.
7. The trees and clouds that made up the ________________ looked real in the film.
8. The ________________ behind the fish looked so realistic in the animated film.
9. The animator made a ________________ model of the elephant to use in the film.
10. One animated film showed dinosaurs and other animals from ________________ times.

Directions Choose two of the vocabulary words and write a sentence for each one.

11. ____

____

12. ____

____

Journey to the New World

5.4.1

DRAW CONCLUSIONS
QUESTIONING

SUMMARY Jane and her family emigrate with other English families to England's first American colony at Roanoke. They plan to join earlier colonists who settled there, but find the colony deserted. Thanks to a lot of hard work and a friendly encounter with an Indian girl, Jane and her family hope the colony will survive.

LESSON VOCABULARY

blunders	civilization
complex	envy
fleeing	inspired
rustling	strategy

INTRODUCE THE BOOK

INTRODUCE THE TITLE AND AUTHOR Discuss with students the title and the author of *Journey to the New World.* Based on the title and the title page illustration, ask them to say what they think the book will be about. Ask them to explain what historical fiction means.

BUILD BACKGROUND Invite students to say what they know about the earliest British colonies in America. Ask: "Was it easy for English settlers to adapt to their new environment? What did they have trouble with? What did they need to learn?"

PREVIEW Have students preview the book by looking at the illustrations. Ask students to discuss how these text features give an idea of what this book will be about. Ask what they think they will learn from this book.

READ THE BOOK

SET PURPOSE Have students set a purpose for reading *Journey to the New World.* Students' interest in what life was like in Roanoke colony should guide this purpose.

STRATEGY SUPPORT: QUESTIONING As students preview the book, have them think of questions they might ask about the text and illustrations, such as, "Why are the people in the illustrations dressed like this?" Explain that when readers ask questions, they can then read on to find the answers.

COMPREHENSION QUESTIONS

PAGE 5 How does Jane feel about journeying to the New World? *(She's scared.)*

PAGE 7 What does Jane's dream foreshadow? *(hints that Roanoke colony may not be successful)*

PAGE 10 How long was the journey from England to Virginia? *(three months at sea)*

PAGE 15 What conclusion can you draw about Governor White and his leadership abilities? *(He is a good leader who thinks of practical solutions and tries to remain optimistic.)*

PAGE 17 Why was it so important for the settlers to get crops planted? *(needed to get seeds in the ground before planting season was over)*

PAGE 25 What did Jane know about raspberries? *(She knew they were edible because she had seen them back in Portsmouth but she had never eaten one because they were too expensive.)*

REVISIT THE BOOK

READER RESPONSE

1. Students might say the soldiers fought with the Indians or joined a group of Indians.
2. Responses will vary.
3. Acceptable answers: civil, civics, civilian, city.
4. Students might say that they would have brought the other settlers back to the ship, and had them return to England.

EXTEND UNDERSTANDING Have students comment on the illustrations in the selection. What details about life in Roanoke can they learn from the illustrations? What other illustrations would they like to see?

RESPONSE OPTIONS

WRITING Invite students to write a journal entry from the point of view of one of the characters from the story. Challenge them to use some of the vocabulary words in their journal entry.

ELL Invite students to make a dictionary entry or bilingual glossary for each of the vocabulary words. Have them include the sentences they write for each word in their entries or glossaries.

SOCIAL STUDIES CONNECTION

Time For SOCIAL STUDIES

Students can learn more about Roanoke Colony by going to the library or using the Internet. Challenge them to find out more about the Croatoan Indians who lived in the area.

Skill Work

TEACH/REVIEW VOCABULARY

Invite students to use each of the vocabulary words in a sentence. Challenge them to write sentences related to the selection.

TARGET SKILL AND STRATEGY

DRAW CONCLUSIONS Remind students that drawing conclusions means making sensible decisions or forming reasonable opinions after thinking about the facts and details in what you are reading. Challenge students to jot down notes as they read about possible conclusions they may be able to draw after completing the reading. Challenge them to test their conclusions when they finish reading. Have them ask: Are my conclusions valid? What details support them?

QUESTIONING As students read, encourage them to pause every so often to ask questions about the text. Have students create a T-chart of questions as they read. As they find the answers, have them record them in the second column. Explain that asking and answering questions will help them better understand what they are reading.

ADDITIONAL SKILL INSTRUCTION

PLOT Remind students that the plot is an organized pattern of events. The organization is often sequential, but authors may also introduce flashbacks, which interrupt the story to tell about something that happened in the past, and with foreshadowing, which hints at events to come. Challenge students to use a graphic organizer to track the plot of the story. Invite them to look for flashbacks and foreshadowing.

Name____

Draw Conclusions

- A **conclusion** is a sensible decision you reach after you think about details or facts in what you read.
- **Drawing conclusions** means to make sensible decisions or form reasonable opinions after thinking about the details or facts in what you read.

Directions Read the paragraph below. Then, answer the questions that follow.

Jane and the other passengers also took comfort from the fact that they would be greeted by a small group of English soldiers when they arrived at Roanoke. During the previous year, a large group of colonists had left Roanoke and returned to England after running low on supplies and encountering difficulties with the local Indians. The leaders of Roanoke wouldn't allow the island to be totally abandoned, so they had a dozen soldiers sent over from England to guard the settlement until Jane's family and everyone else arrived.

1. What conclusion can you draw about the new colonists' expectations about Roanoke?

____

2. Give two facts or details to support your conclusion.

____

____

3. What conclusion can you draw about why the first group of colonists returned to England?

____

____

4. Give two facts or details to support your conclusion.

____

____

5. Write a well-supported conclusion about how Jane and her family might have felt differently about their plans if they had known what awaited them.

____

____

____

Name ______________________________

Vocabulary

Directions Read each sentence. Write the word from the box that fits correctly in each sentence. Some words may be used more than once.

Check the Words You Know

___blunders	___civilization	___complex	___envy
___fleeing	___inspired	___rustling	___strategy

1. Jane and her family, like many others, were ______________ economic hardships in England.
2. They were ______________ by stories they heard of a new colony in Virginia, where the climate was good and the land was fertile.
3. Queen Elizabeth's ______________ for England's future was to build colonies in the New World.
4. The relationship between the early colonists and the local Indians was very ______________.
5. The English believed their own ______________ was more advanced than the Indians' way of life.
6. The English colonists hoped to avoid repeating the ______________ of the earlier settlers.
7. They did not ______________ the fate of the earlier colonists.
8. Instead, they listened to Governor White's passionate speech and were ______________ by it.
9. The colonists' ______________ was to first build themselves shelters, and then get some crops planted.
10. As the wind gently blew through the ______________ bushes, Jane peeked out at the Indian village.

Wilma Rudolph: Running to Win

5.4.2

GENERALIZE

PREDICT AND SET PURPOSE

SUMMARY This expository nonfiction selection describes the many challenges Wilma Rudolph faced from the day she was born until the day she won three Olympic gold medals.

LESSON VOCABULARY

Dalmatian	frilly
promenading	sprained
substitute	

INTRODUCE THE BOOK

INTRODUCE THE TITLE AND AUTHOR Discuss the title and author of *Wilma Rudolph: Running to Win*. Ask students if they have heard of Wilma Rudolph. Discuss what they already know about her. Have students look at the cover photograph. Ask: What do you think these runners are trying to do? Why? Which runner do you think is Wilma Rudolph?

BUILD BACKGROUND Ask students if they have ever faced a challenge. Have students share their experiences. Discuss the challenges people faced years ago before vaccinations were made and technology had developed. Ask: How do you think someone can get past a challenge?

PREVIEW/USE TEXT FEATURES Have students look at all of the photographs and read the captions in the book. Discuss how the captions help them know what the photographs are about. Ask: How will the pictures help you understand the story? What do the captions tell you about what you're going to read?

READ THE BOOK

SET PURPOSE Have students set a purpose for reading *Wilma Rudolph: Running to Win*. As students read, have them list the various challenges that Wilma faced. Have students think about how Wilma overcame the challenges in her life.

STRATEGY SUPPORT: PREDICT AND SET PURPOSE As students read, have them write predictions and then write the information that proved their predictions. After reading, have students share their predictions and proven information.

COMPREHENSION QUESTIONS

PAGE 4 What were the types of challenges Wilma faced from the beginning of her life? *(illnesses; premature birth, pneumonia, whooping cough, measles, chicken pox, scarlet fever)*

PAGES 5–6 What generalization can you make about how African American people were treated in the past? *(Responses may vary but make sure students understand the concept of segregation.)*

PAGE 8 Based on the chapter title, what do you predict Wilma will do? *(walk by herself; will become a famous athlete)*

PAGE 12 Why do you think the author says, "Wilma would have reason to remember that conversation later on"? *(Responses may vary but make sure students understand the concept of author's purpose)*

PAGE 23 How did Wilma "live on" after her death in 1994? *(inspiring many young people, especially African American girls, to work hard and follow their dreams)*

REVISIT THE BOOK

READER RESPONSE

1. Responses may vary but make sure students understand the concept of generalization.
2. Responses may vary but make sure students relate their responses to Wilma Rudolph.
3. Responses may vary but make sure students show understanding of what each vocabulary word means.
4. Responses may vary but make sure students understand the concept of *challenge*.

EXTEND UNDERSTANDING Explain to students that back when Wilma was a child, there were no vaccinations to protect people from diseases such as polio. Discuss the benefits of vaccinations today.

RESPONSE OPTIONS

WRITING Have students write their own story (real or fiction) about a challenge and how they overcame that challenge. Encourage students to be descriptive and realistic.

ELL English Language Learners can act out (Drama) their challenge and how they overcame that challenge. Encourage them to use their English as much as possible while acting.

SOCIAL STUDIES CONNECTION

Have students research about the life of their hero or heroine or another famous person. Have students list the challenges and successes that person faced. Students can look in books or on the internet to gather information.

Skill Work

TEACH/REVIEW VOCABULARY

Review vocabulary words with students. Write each word on a separate card and fold in half. Put cards in a container. One at a time, have students pick a card, give a definition for the word, and use the word in a sentence. If needed, students can find the word in the text and read the sentence from the text before giving a definition. Repeat until all words have been used.

TARGET SKILL AND STRATEGY

GENERALIZE Remind students that sometimes when they read, they are given ideas about several things or people and they can make a statement about all of them together. This statement is called a *generalization*. Valid generalizations are accurate or true based on the information in the story, and faulty generalizations are not. As students read, have them write a generalization about each chapter and include facts that support their generalization.

PREDICT AND SET PURPOSE Remind students that a *prediction* is what you think might happen in a story based on what you have already read or know. Read page 7 with students. Make a prediction about the recovery of Wilma's leg. Then read the first paragraph on page 8. Discuss how predictions can be proven correct or incorrect with new information as they read on.

ADDITIONAL SKILL INSTRUCTION

AUTHOR'S PURPOSE Remind students that authors often write to inform, persuade, express, or entertain. Ask: Why do you think Meish Goldish wrote *Wilma Rudolph: Running to Win*? What in the text makes you think that is the purpose? Have students share their idea of the purpose and examples from the text that support that purpose.

Name ____

Generalize

- When an author presents ideas or facts about several things or people and makes a statement about them all together, this is a **generalization**.
- **Valid generalizations** are based on facts and are accurate; **faulty generalizations** are not.

Directions Using information from *Wilma Rudolph: Running to Win*, write facts about Wilma Rudolph in the ovals on the graphic organizer below. Then write a generalization about Wilma in the center circle.

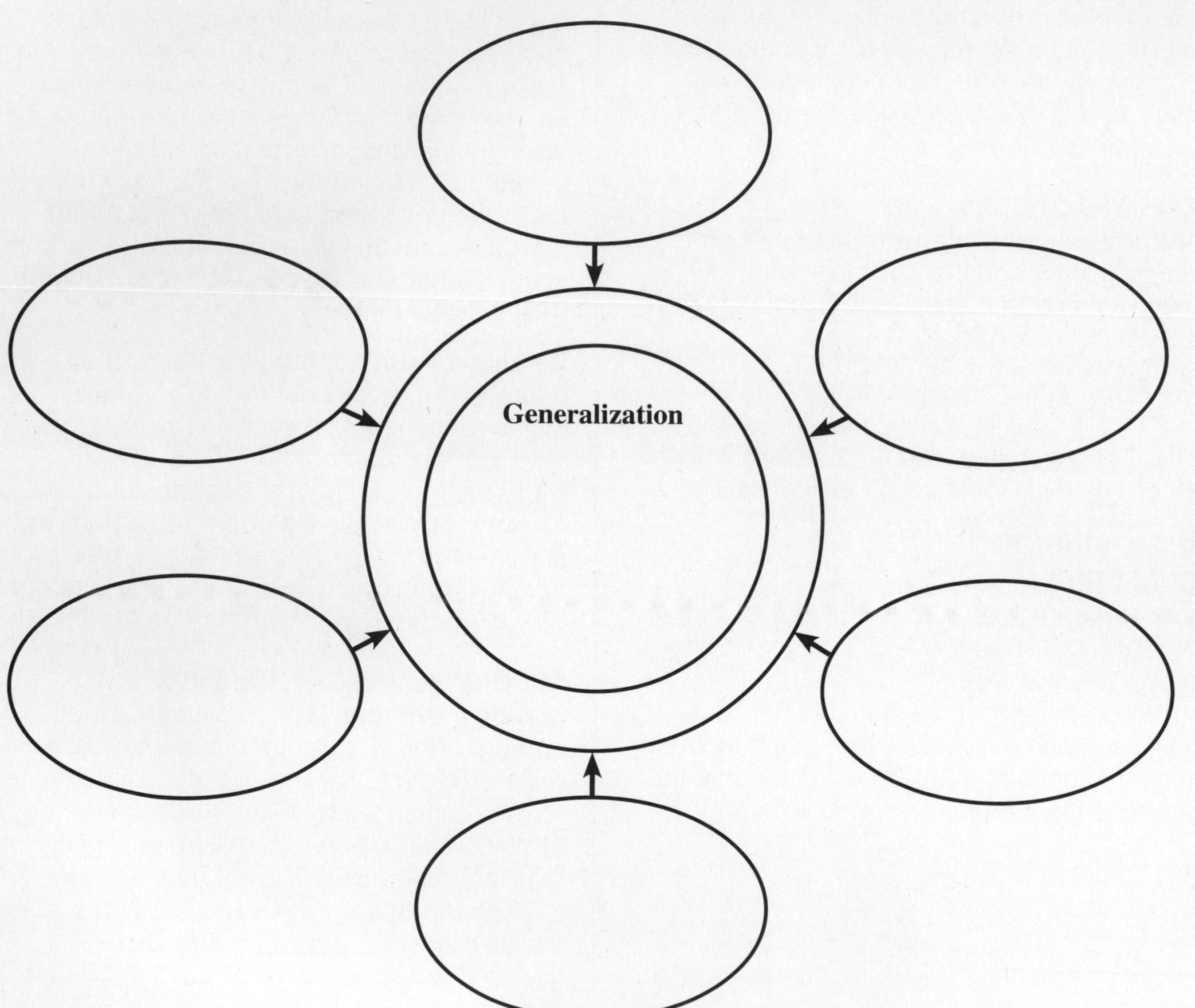

Name ____________________

Vocabulary

Directions Underline the context clue(s) that explains what each of the boldface words mean.

Check the Words You Know

___Dalmatian ___frilly ___promenading
___sprained ___substitute

1. The **Dalmatian** wagged its tail happily as the fireman patted its head.
2. Sue's **frilly** dress was layered with colorful ruffles and lace.
3. Ms. Black's students were **promenading** around the room in their holiday costumes.
4. Jack's ankle was **sprained** when his foot twisted as he fell down the step.
5. I like to **substitute** the sweetness in my tea with honey instead of sugar.

Directions Write your own sentence with context clues for each vocabulary word from the box. Have a partner read your sentences and underline the clues.

6. ____________________
____
7. ____________________
____
8. ____________________
____
9. ____________________
____
10. ____________________
____

Changing for Survival: Bird Adaptations

5.4.3

GRAPHIC SOURCES
IMPORTANT IDEAS

SUMMARY This book surveys various birds from around the world. It identifies and describes different bird groups, including sea birds, shore birds, birds of prey, and song birds. It describes their habitats, eating habits, behavior, and physical make-up.

LESSON VOCABULARY

critical	enable
mucus	scarce
specialize	sterile

INTRODUCE THE BOOK

INTRODUCE THE TITLE AND AUTHOR Discuss with students the title and the author of *Changing for Survival: Bird Adaptations*. Based on the title, ask students what information they think this book will provide.

BUILD BACKGROUND Invite students to share what they know about birds. Ask if anyone has owned a bird. What sorts of bird behaviors have students observed? Ask what it is about birds that students find interesting. Introduce the word "adaptation." Ask students what they think this word means. You may wish to tell them that birds or animals *adapt* by changing or adjusting to a special situation.

ELL Encourage English language learners to share names of birds in their home languages.

PREVIEW/USE TEXT FEATURES Have students look at the photographs, captions, and headings in the book. Ask students what they notice about the way this book is organized. What other text features do the students recognize? How do they think the photographs can help them understand more about what they're reading?

READ THE BOOK

SET PURPOSE Have students set a purpose for reading *Changing for Survival: Bird Adaptations*. Their interest in birds and animals and in environmental issues may drive this purpose. Students may continue to add questions and answers to their KWL charts.

STRATEGY SUPPORT: IMPORTANT IDEAS Remind students that good readers are able to distinguish between important ideas and nonessential details as they read. Explain that important ideas give more information about the topic of the book. As students read, encourage them to look for important ideas and details that support them.

COMPREHENSION QUESTIONS

PAGES 4–5 How have birds evolved into "flying machines"? *(Wings and bodies covered with feathers, lightweight bodies, eat a lot for energy.)*

PAGES 6–7 What do these photos show you? *(Possible responses: Birds live in many different areas. There are many types of birds.)*

PAGES 10–11 What is the main idea? What are the supporting details? *(Shore birds have adapted in different ways to life along the shore. Some have long, pointy beaks for digging and long, thin legs to keep bodies above water. Others have short beaks and legs because they eat above the water.)*

PAGE 14 What are some of the owl's special adaptations? *(Possible responses: Nocturnal, huge eyes in front of face, can rotate head almost all the way around, soft feathers help make them silent flyers.)*

PAGE 22 What are some challenges that birds face? *(Possible responses: growing cities, pollution, cutting down forests, destroyed habitat)*

REVISIT THE BOOK

READER RESPONSE

1. The author uses each caption as a heading for the pages that follow.
2. Possible response: Birds adapt in order to survive in their habitats. This important idea helped me to identify the ways that they adapt.
3. Thick, sticky liquid; makes insects stick to tongue.
4. Responses will vary.

EXTEND UNDERSTANDING Have students think about what their understanding of this text would be like if the book contained no photographs. Discuss how the photographs help make some of the points presented in the text much more vivid.

RESPONSE OPTIONS

WRITING Encourage students to pick a favorite bird from *Changing for Survival.* Have them write a poem about the bird. They should include facts they learned from the book in their poems.

SCIENCE CONNECTION

TIME FOR Science

How have other animals adapted to their environments? Have students choose an animal to research. Encourage them to pay special attention to how the animal has adapted to its habitat.

Skill Work

TEACH/REVIEW VOCABULARY

Have students locate the vocabulary words in the text. Have them define each word using context clues, the glossary, and a dictionary. Then, invite students to list for each word as many words as possible that have similar meanings or are related in some way.

TARGET SKILL AND STRATEGY

GRAPHIC SOURCES Remind students that *graphic sources* are graphs, maps, pictures, photographs, and diagrams that help strengthen their understanding of the text. Students may also use graphic sources before reading to predict and preview information. Have students create a KWL chart. They should list what they already know about birds and what they want to know.

IMPORTANT IDEAS Review with students that *important ideas* tell more about the main idea or topic of the book. Ask: What is the main idea of this book? What are important ideas that tell more about it? Use a Web graphic organizer to list students' answers on the board.

ADDITIONAL SKILL INSTRUCTION

FACT AND OPINION A *statement of fact* can be proven true or false by reading, observing, or asking an expert. A *statement of opinion* is a judgment or belief that cannot be proven true or false but can be supported or explained. Help students make distinctions between the two types by reading aloud statements from the book. Challenge students to identify what types of statement they are.

Name ____

Graphic Sources

Graphic sources are graphs, maps, pictures, photographs, and diagrams that help strengthen understanding of text.

Directions On the map below, show the ranges of penguins, jacanas, great white pelicans, red-tailed hawks, ostriches, and ruby-throated hummingbirds you learned about in the book. Include a title and key.

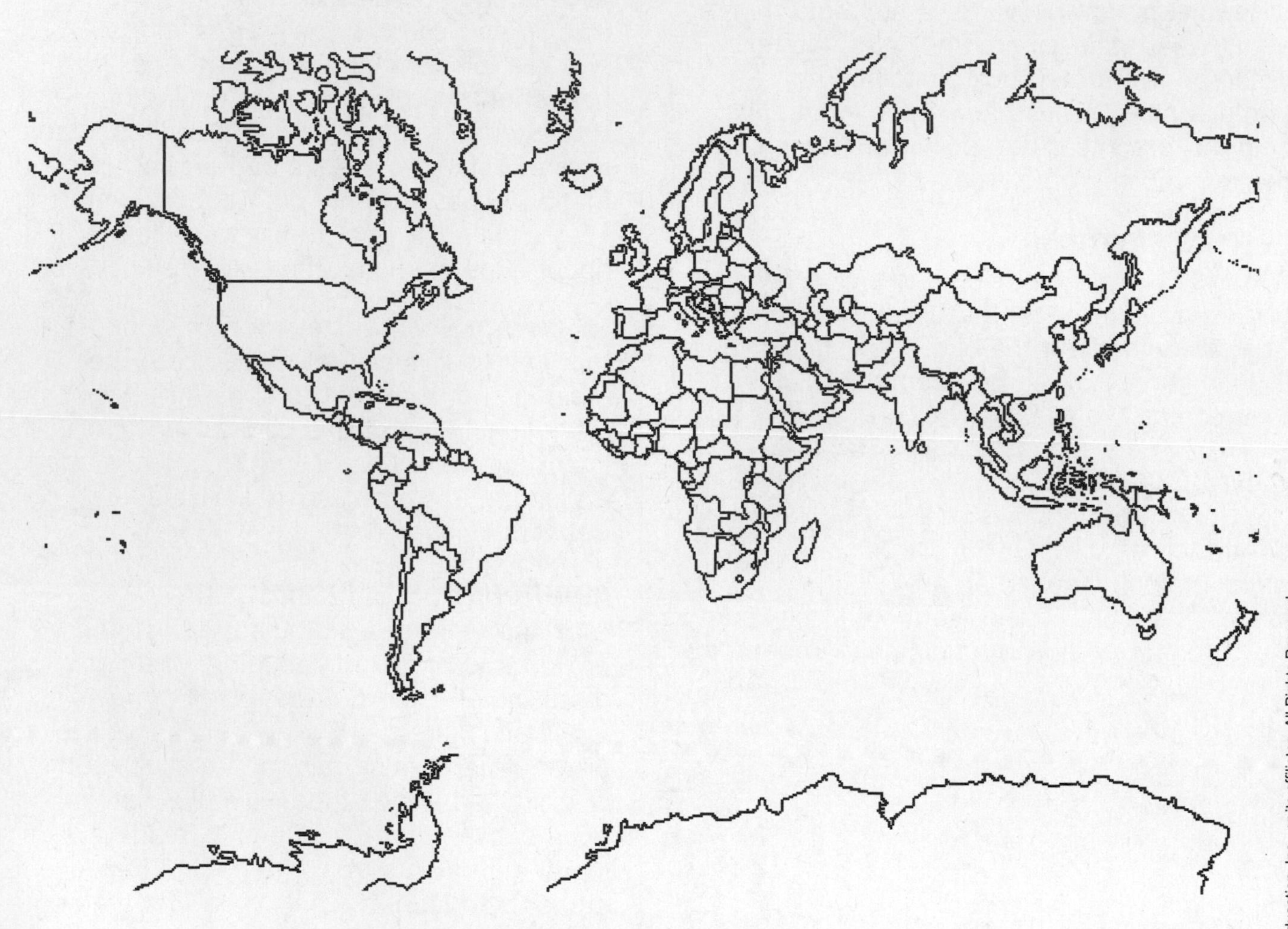

Name ______________________________

Vocabulary

Directions Fill in the blank spaces in each sentence below with the correct word from the "Words You Know" box and an appropriate word from the "Birds to Know" box. You may refer to your reader for information about the birds.

Check the Words You Know

- ___critical
- ___enable
- ___mucus
- ___scarce
- ___specialize
- ___sterile

1. ________________ have a special ________________ on their tongues for snatching up insects to eat.

2. ________________ live in an environment where food is ________________. They have to walk a long way in search of food.

3. ________________ have adapted flippers in place of wings that ________________ them to swim underwater.

4. The ________________ has the longest beak of any bird. It allows it to ________________ in fishing by scooping fish from the water.

5. Scientists who work with baby birds keep them in a ________________ environment so they stay healthy.

6. When birds are endangered, bird conservationists feel it is ________________ to help save them.

The New Kid at School

5.4.4

GENERALIZE
TEXT STRUCTURE

SUMMARY This nonfiction selection is about what it is like to be the new student at school. It provides a lot of good suggestions of what new students can do to make the transition to a new school less difficult. It also talks about what other students can do to welcome the new student.

LESSON VOCABULARY

cavities	combination
demonstrates	episode
profile	strict

INTRODUCE THE BOOK

INTRODUCE THE TITLE AND AUTHOR Discuss with students the title and author of *The New Kid at School*. Based on the title, ask students what kind of information they think this book will provide. Direct students to look at the cover photo to see if they can guess more clues about the selection's content.

BUILD BACKGROUND Ask students if they have ever been the new kid at school. If not, have they ever helped a new kid trying to fit in at a new school? Discuss some of the things they did as a new student to make friends and fit in. Also discuss things they did to make a new student feel more at home.

ELL Ask students what it felt like for them on the first day at a new school. What did they do to try to make friends?

PREVIEW/USE TEXT FEATURES Have students look through the book at all the photos. Ask students how the photos give clues to what is going to happen in the book.

READ THE BOOK

SET PURPOSE Have students set a purpose for reading *The New Kid at School*. Students may want to focus on Marcus and his problems at the new school. Or they may want to focus on what the other students do to help him feel at home.

STRATEGY SUPPORT: TEXT STRUCTURE As students read, recognizing a text's structure or organization of ideas will help them with comprehension. Graphic organizers such as story maps, webs, or charts can help students keep track of important ideas. Give students practice in using a graphic organizer by having them make a problem/solution chart that lists the problems faced by a new kid at school as they are described in the book. For each problem, students should identify the solution that is offered in the text. Explain to students that they can use their completed graphic organizers to remind them of what they learned by reading *The New Kid at School.*

COMPREHENSION QUESTIONS

PAGE 6 What are some simple things you can do to make a new student feel at home? *(Responses may vary: say hello, strike up a conversation.)*

PAGE 6 What are some different feelings that might be a reaction to change? *(Responses may vary: excited, nervous.)*

PAGE 12 In addition to changing schools, what major change is Marcus having to get used to? *(Responses may vary, but may include moving from a house to an apartment, getting to know a whole new town.)*

PAGE 15 What are some of the ways you can say goodbye? *(Responses may vary, but may include: say good-bye to friends and teachers, take photos and mementos with you.)*

REVISIT THE BOOK

READER RESPONSE

1. Responses will vary, but may include: A new student will feel nervous and alone. She/he might not know where things are in the school. She/he might be having problems at home that have caused the move. The new student might want to find out how to continue activities she/he did at the old school or might want to use the opportunity to try completely new things.
2. Possible responses: What he or she can do: pursue a favorite activity, be yourself, expect ups and downs. What we can do: introduce yourself, start a conversation, create a welcome gift, be a mentor, share insider information.
3. Answers will vary.
4. Possible responses: Pursue activities you enjoy, expect ups and downs, be yourself.

EXTEND UNDERSTANDING Have students read the eight section headings in the book. Ask: How can the headings help you find information quickly? Have students use each heading to explain what each section is all about. For example, for the first heading, students might answer, "This section is all about how to help a new kid by introducing yourself."

RESPONSE OPTIONS

WRITING Have the students write a brief essay about how to help a new kid at their school. Have them imagine that they are sitting down to start the day's history class when the teacher introduces a new student. What might each student do to help the new student feel more at home? What kinds of questions would be good to ask the new student?

SOCIAL STUDIES CONNECTION

Time For SOCIAL STUDIES

Have the class brainstorm about what could go in a welcome bag for a new student like the one discussed in the book on page 10. Have the class create such a welcome kit and give it to the next new student who joins the class.

Skill Work

TEACH/REVIEW VOCABULARY

Review the vocabulary words. Then play "Vocabulary Master" with students. Give students three different definitions for each vocabulary word, including one that is fantastical or silly, and have them select the correct definition and then use the word in a sentence.

TARGET SKILL AND STRATEGY

GENERALIZE Tell students that sometimes when you read, you are given ideas about things or people, and you can make a statement about all of them together. This statement is called a *generalization*. Look for clue words, such as *most, always, all,* and *never.* Valid generalizations are accurate. Faulty generalizations are not accurate. Tell them that identifying faulty generalizations can help tell whether an author is biased. After reading, have students make their own generalization by asking them to generalize about new kids at school. (*All new students face problems at a new school.*)

TEXT STRUCTURE Reinforce to students that recognizing text structure is the ability to recognize the organization of a piece of writing. As students read *The New Kid at School,* have them answer questions in a graphic organizer with the headings Problems and Solutions. What is the problem? Who is trying to solve the problem? How did the problem get solved? Is the problem solved? Why or why not?

ADDITIONAL SKILL INSTRUCTION

CAUSE AND EFFECT Remind students that a *cause* is why something happened, and an *effect* is what happened. Point out that causes and effects are sometimes not obvious in the text, and sometimes there are multiple causes for the same effect. As students read, have them ask themselves: Why was Marcus worried on his first day in his new school?

Name ______________________________

Generalize

- A **generalization** is a broad statement or rule that applies to many examples. A generalization is made after thinking about a number of examples or facts and what they have in common.

Directions Reread the following passage from *The New Kid at School.*

About his first day, Marcus says, "I was worried about a lot of things. The new school was much bigger than my old one, and I was scared of getting lost. I wondered if my new teacher would be strict or nice. I was afraid I would never make new friends or that other kids might be mean to me."

Directions Answer the questions below.

1. When we are afraid, we often make generalizations about the future. What generalizations does Marcus make about the other students at his new school?

____

2. List another fear Marcus has about his new school.

____

3. List another fear Marcus has about his new school.

____

4. List another fear Marcus has about his new school.

____

5. What if Marcus could turn these negative expectations around? What would be a more positive generalization he could make about his fellow students?

____

6. How might you turn around the fear you listed in question 2?

____

7. How might you turn around the fear you listed in question 3?

____

8. How might you turn around the fear listed in question 4?

____

Name______________________________________

Vocabulary

Directions Complete each sentence with a word from the box.

Check the Words You Know

___ cavities	___ combination
___ demonstrates	___ episode
___ profile	___ strict

1. Marcus was afraid that his teacher would be ______________ .
2. The teacher told them to watch tonight's ______________ of *Star Trek*.
3. Marcus's new school was a ______________ of old and new.
4. The bulletin board in art class ______________ the students' artistic talents.
5. Marcus had not had ______________ for three years.
6. The art teacher traced his ______________ on a piece of paper.

Directions Write a brief paragraph discussing Marcus's first day at school, using as many vocabulary words as possible.

____
____
____
____
____
____
____
____
____
____
____
____

Strange Sports with Weird Gear

5.4.5

DRAW CONCLUSIONS
VISUALIZE

SUMMARY This book discusses strange sports that use unusual gear. It describes the sports of curling, rhythmic gymnastics, and jai alai.

LESSON VOCABULARY

bluish	cartwheels
gymnastics	hesitation
limelight	skidded
somersault	throbbing
wincing	

INTRODUCE THE BOOK

INTRODUCE THE TITLE AND AUTHOR Discuss with students the title and the author of *Strange Sports with Weird Gear*. Based on the photos, ask students what kind of information they think this book will provide.

BUILD BACKGROUND Discuss students' favorite sports. Ask them to name some unusual sports they know and describe why they think they are unusual.

ELL Ask students to describe a favorite sport that is popular in their culture. Ask them to describe how the sport is played and tell if there is anything unusual about it.

PREVIEW/USE TEXT FEATURES As students preview the book, action shots of sports will probably immediately attract their interest. Have students look at the photographs and read the captions. Ask them how the photographs help them visualize what the author is describing.

READ THE BOOK

SET PURPOSE Have students set a purpose for reading *Strange Sports with Weird Gear*. Keeping the author's purpose in mind should guide this idea.

STRATEGY SUPPORT: VISUALIZE As students read about unusual sports, visualizing gives them a chance to combine what they already know about sports with the new information about sports in this book. Visualizing can also help them compare and contrast different sports.

COMPREHENSION QUESTIONS

PAGE 11 What conclusions can you draw about why changes in curling were made? *(Changes were made because the curling stone used to be very heavy and hard to get down the ice. It was hard on the players.)*

PAGE 12 What are the two main parts of rhythmic gymnastics? *(dancing and gymnastics)*

PAGES 14–17 What gear is used in rhythmic gymnastics? *(Possible responses: hoops, balls, rope with knots at each end, clubs, ribbons)*

PAGE 23 What gear do jai alai players use or wear? *(wooden basket, leather gloves, and a helmet)*

REVISIT THE BOOK

READER RESPONSE

1. Jai alai, curling, rhythmic gymnastics
2. Jai alai, because of the crack of the ball against the wall and baskets
3. The suffix changes the meaning of each word by converting an action verb to an adjective.
4. Responses will vary.

EXTEND UNDERSTANDING As students look at the photographs, ask them why certain photos interest them more than others. Ask students how specific photographs aid in their understanding of the text.

RESPONSE OPTIONS

WRITING Suggest that students choose one of the sports in this book and imagine what it would be like to play it. Have them write a brief description of the experience using vivid details.

SOCIAL STUDIES CONNECTION

Time For SOCIAL STUDIES

Students can learn more about these or other sports that interest them by researching them on the Internet or at the library.

Skill Work

TEACH/REVIEW VOCABULARY

Divide students into small groups. Have each group write a funny sentence using each vocabulary word corrcctly. Then have each group read its sentences, leaving out the vocabulary word. Have other groups race to find which vocabulary word fits into the sentence.

TARGET SKILL AND STRATEGY

DRAW CONCLUSIONS Remind students that a *conclusion* is a sensible decision reached after thinking about details or facts in what is read. As they read, have students write down important details about each sport. Ask them to draw conclusions about each sport based on the facts.

VISUALIZE Remind students that to *visualize* is to create a picture in the mind. As students read, suggest that they visualize what it would be like to play each sport.

ADDITIONAL SKILL INSTRUCTION

COMPARE AND CONTRAST Remind students that to compare and contrast things means to look for how they are alike and different. Have students read page 11 to compare and contrast curling. Students also can compare information in the book to their own knowledge.

Name ______________________

Draw Conclusions

A **conclusion** is a sensible decision reached after thinking about details or facts in what is read.

Directions Based on the equipment used in each sport, answer the following questions.

1. Does curling take a lot of strength? Why or why not?

____

____

2. Are rhythmic gymnasts hurt easily? Why or why not?

____

____

3. Can jai alai be dangerous? Why or why not?

____

____

4. Why are the ropes used by rhythmic gymnasts often made to look like snakes?

____

____

5. Which of the three sports would you like to try? Why?

____

____

Name____

Vocabulary

Directions Write the word from the box that best matches each definition.

Check the Words You Know

- ___bluish
- ___gymnastics
- ___limelight
- ___somersault
- ___wincing
- ___cartwheels
- ___hesitation
- ___skidded
- ___throbbing

1. the focus of attention ____________________
2. a touch of blue ____________________
3. exercises that use strength, agility, and coordination ____________________
4. shrinking one's face or body in pain or disgust ____________________
5. slid ____________________
6. rolling over by turning heels over head ____________________
7. a pause ____________________
8. sideways handsprings ____________________
9. pulsating or beating strongly ____________________

10. Write a sentence using any vocabulary word from the box.

____

____

Bill Lucks Out

PLOT AND CHARACTER
PRIOR KNOWLEDGE

SUMMARY Fifth-grader Bill Harrison scores a double play when he makes the majors in the Little League tryouts and scores an A on his research project. For his project, he must interview someone with first-hand knowledge of the Vietnam War. An older man in the neighborhood who acts a little oddly turns out to be a Vietnam veteran with a lot of interesting stories to tell. It also turns out that he and Bill share another interest—baseball.

LESSON VOCABULARY

abandoned	attempts	savage
bellowed	cavern	
feat	immensely	

INTRODUCE THE BOOK

INTRODUCE THE TITLE AND AUTHOR Discuss with students the title and the author of *Bill Lucks Out*. Based on the title, ask students to say what they think the book will be about.

BUILD BACKGROUND Discuss what students know about the Vietnam War. Ask if they know when it was, and if they know any Vietnam veterans.

PREVIEW/USE TEXT FEATURES As students preview the book, invite them to notice the illustrations. Draw their attention to the map on page 15, and the photo on page 32. Explain that these text features give the reader different kinds of information about the story.

READ THE BOOK

SET PURPOSE Have students set a purpose for reading *Bill Lucks Out*. Students' interest in baseball and the war in Vietnam should guide this purpose. Ask students to think about the difference between researching a topic in the library and interviewing a person with first-hand knowledge.

STRATEGY SUPPORT: PRIOR KNOWLEDGE Have readers write down what they know about the Vietnam War before they start the book. Have them add new information as they read.

COMPREHENSION QUESTIONS

PAGE 5 What is the first problem that seems to occupy Bill Harrison's mind? *(getting into the majors in Little League)*

PAGE 6 What details does the author give that make the man mowing the lawn seem a little odd? *(has a long gray beard that seems out of place in the neighborhood, walks backwards and pushes lawnmower behind him, Rob's mom says he's crazy, Craig's dad says he is sick)*

PAGE 11 What are the two parts of the research assignment? *(Part 1: what students learned from books; Part 2: what it was like to really be there)*

PAGE 14 Why did President Kennedy send troops to Vietnam in 1961? *(The U.S. didn't want the Communists in the north to rule all of Vietnam.)*

PAGE 25 How did Mr. Jenkins's war stories change Bill's idea of war? *(Possible response: Jenkins made him see that war is hard, dangerous, and not a lot of fun.)*

PAGE 27 What common interests do Bill and Mr. Jenkins have? *(baseball)*

REVISIT THE BOOK

READER RESPONSE

1. Bill comes to like Mr. Jenkins instead of thinking he is strange. Bill tells his friends that Mr. Jenkins is a nice person instead of sharing their poor opinion of him as he did before.
2. Responses will vary.
3. Possible response: *spectacle:* event, eyeglasses; *prospect:* possibility, extensive view; *pilot:* a person who flies an aircraft, to act as a guide to. The first definition of each word applies in the selection.
4. Responses will vary.

EXTEND UNDERSTANDING Have students look again at the map on page 15. Ask them to describe the location of Vietnam. Have them look again at the photo on page 32. Ask: How do you think the people in this photo felt? Why?

RESPONSE OPTIONS

WRITING Suggest that students write one paragraph from Bill's point of view, and one paragraph from Mr. Jenkins's point of view about their first meeting.

SOCIAL STUDIES CONNECTION

Time For SOCIAL STUDIES

Students can learn about the Vietnam Veterans Memorial in Washington, D.C., by using the Internet or going to the library. Suggest they find out about Maya Lin, who designed the memorial, or read the accounts of veterans who have visited the memorial. Have students tell about their research.

Skill Work

TEACH/REVIEW VOCABULARY

Have students find the word *savage* on page 25. Ask: What is a synonym for *savage?* Continue in a similar fashion with the remaining vocabulary words.

TARGET SKILL AND STRATEGY

PLOT AND CHARACTER Remind students that the *plot* is a pattern of events, usually organized around a problem or conflict. Explain that *characters* are the people in stories. Authors usually tell what their characters look like, how they act, and what kind of people they are. As they read, have students think about the plot. Ask: What happens at the beginning, middle, and end of the story? Ask: Do any of the characters change? How?

ELL Have students list the characters in the book. Have them brainstorm words that describe each character, and list them under each character's name. Have them read the list of words for each character and choose the word that best describes each person.

PRIOR KNOWLEDGE Remind students that *prior knowledge* is what a reader knows about a given topic gathered from reading and personal experience. Active readers add to and revise their prior knowledge as they read. Ask students to tell their prior knowledge about the Vietnam War. Ask them to keep track of new things they learn about the war as they read the selection. Have them think about the role the Vietnam War plays in the development of the plot of the book. How does learning about the war affect the main character?

ADDITIONAL SKILL INSTRUCTION

CAUSE AND EFFECT Remind students that *cause* is defined as "why something happened." *Effect* is defined as "what happened." Explain that sometimes, clue words such as *because*, *so*, and *since* indicate a relationship between why something happened and what happened. Have students be aware of what happens in the plot and why characters react as they do.

Name ____________________

Plot and Character

- The **plot** is a pattern of events usually organized around a problem or conflict.
- A **character** is a person who takes part in the events of a story.

Directions Fill in the graphic organizer below about *Bill Lucks Out*.

Title ____________________

Characters

Setting

Problem

Events

____

____

____

____

____

____

____

Solution

Name ____

Vocabulary

Directions Draw a line from each word to its definition.

Check the Words You Know

___abandoned ___attempts ___bellowed ___cavern
___feat ___immensely ___savage

1. abandoned — **a.** endeavors
2. attempts — **b.** deserted
3. bellowed — **c.** shouted loudly
4. cavern — **d.** not civilized
5. feat — **e.** an act showing great skill
6. immensely — **f.** a large cave
7. savage — **g.** very greatly

Directions Write a paragraph about *Bill Lucks Out*. Use as many vocabulary words as you can.

____
____
____
____
____
____
____
____
____
____
____
____

Explore with Science

GRAPHIC SOURCES
INFERRING

SUMMARY Explorers and scientists who travel to extreme places such as Mount Everest and Antarctica rely on technology to help them get there and back. They also use technology to study and learn about these extreme environments.

LESSON VOCABULARY

cramped	debris
interior	ooze
robotic	sediment
sonar	

INTRODUCE THE BOOK

INTRODUCE THE TITLE AND AUTHOR Discuss with students the title and the author of *Explore with Science*. Based on the title, ask students to say what they think the book will be about. Bring their attention to the cover photo. Ask: What is one place the book might discuss?

BUILD BACKGROUND Discuss what students know about the kinds of technology that might be used in exploring extreme places. Ask them to list some places they think might be very challenging to explore. Have them discuss the challenges faced by people who go there.

PREVIEW/USE TEXT FEATURES As students preview the book, the photos and illustrations will probably attract their attention. Suggest that students also notice diagrams, labels, and heads.

READ THE BOOK

SET PURPOSE Have students set a purpose for reading *Explore with Science*. Students' interest in expeditions to extreme places such as Mount Everest and Antarctica should guide this purpose. Suggest that students think about the most modern kinds of technology that scientists and explorers might take with them on expeditions to extreme places.

STRATEGY SUPPORT: INFERRING Remind students that when we *infer*, we use what we already know about a topic combined with information from the text to come up with our own ideas about the text or story. As students read, have them note clues from the text that they think will help them infer how technology makes exploring easier.

COMPREHENSION QUESTIONS

PAGE 4 Who was Sir George Everest? *(the man who mapped the Himalayan Mountains, where Mt. Everest stands)*

PAGE 6 What technology did Professor Bradford Washburn use to measure the height of Mount Everest? *(radar and global positioning satellites)*

PAGE 8 How do satellite phones work? *(They send and receive signals from satellites orbiting the Earth.)*

PAGE 10 What is an altimeter? How is it worn by climbers? What else do they use it for? *(a device that shows height above sea level; worn like a watch; includes a barometer to track changes in weather)*

PAGE 12 What happens when someone climbs too high too quickly? (*Person gets Acute Mountain Sickness, AMS.*)

PAGE 16 What was the Antarctic Treaty? *(In 1959, twelve nations agreed that Antarctica would be used for research.)*

REVISIT THE BOOK

READER RESPONSE

1. Everest, K2, Kangchenjunga, and Lhotse
2. Responses will vary.
3. Possible responses: wreckage, remains, fragments, rubble, rubbish, garbage, trash, waste; She pulled her purse from the wreckage. Please take out the garbage. Nuclear waste is a threat to the environment.
4. Possible responses: What was the first thing you did when you arrived at the top? How did you feel?

EXTEND UNDERSTANDING As students look at the photo of the McMurdo Station on pages 16 and 17, ask what they think it would be like to live there. Have students discuss in pairs what they think some of the hardships of living at McMurdo Station would be. Have them say what they think would be some of the fun things about living there. Have them share their ideas with the class.

RESPONSE OPTIONS

WRITING Suggest that students write two paragraphs about how modern technology is used in modern scientific exploration.

SCIENCE CONNECTION

TIME FOR Science

Students can learn more about the McMurdo Station by researching on the Internet or going to the library. Suggest they learn more about the kinds of research being conducted there. They can take a virtual tour at http://astro.uchicago.edu/cara/vtour/mcmurdo/.

Skill Work

TEACH/REVIEW VOCABULARY

To reinforce the meaning of *debris*, read the third paragraph on page 4. Ask students to say what they think *debris* means. If they are not sure, have them look up the word in a dictionary. Continue in a similar fashion with the remaining vocabulary words.

TARGET SKILL AND STRATEGY

GRAPHIC SOURCES Ask: What graphic sources are in this book? *(captions, headings, sidebars, maps, pictures)* How do these help you as you read? *(Possible responses: They draw attention to important information. They visually show me details from the text.)*

INFERRING Remind students that to *infer*, you combine what you know with text clues to come up with your own ideas. Have students infer one thing about scientists in Antarctica and marine biologists.

ELL Have lower-proficiency students dictate three questions about the selection to higher-proficiency students. Have them work together to find the answers to the questions in the book. Then have them present their questions and answers in pairs.

ADDITIONAL SKILL INSTRUCTION

CAUSE AND EFFECT Remind students that sometimes there can be multiple causes for something and one effect, or one single cause and multiple effects. Invite students to make a chart with two columns. Label one column "Why Something Happened," and the other column "What Happened." Encourage them to fill in the chart as they read the selection.

Name ____________________

Graphic Sources

- **Graphic sources** are graphs, maps, pictures, photographs, charts, and diagrams that help strengthen one's understanding of the text.

Directions Use the graphic sources from *Explore with Science* to answer the questions.

1. What does the caption on page 3 explain about the picture?

2. Using the chart on page 5, what is the fifth tallest mountain? What is its height in feet?

3. According to the map on page 15, which three places show the most mountains without snow cover?

4. Look at the photo on page 20. How are these biologists able to remain underwater?

Name____

Vocabulary

Directions Draw a line from each word to its definition.

Check the Words You Know

___cramped ___debris ___interior ___ooze
___robotic ___sediment ___sonar

1. cramped
2. debris
3. interior
4. ooze
5. robotic
6. sediment
7. sonar

a. very soft and slimy mud
b. tightly crowded and close together
c. dirt, rocks, and sand that have been moved and dropped by wind, water, or ice
d. the most remote, inner area
e. a system that uses sound waves to find objects underwater
f. pieces of broken materials, which are scattered over an area
g. a robot-controlled device, such as an arm

Directions Write a paragraph about *Explore with Science.* Use as many vocabulary words as you can.

____
____
____
____
____
____
____
____
____
____
____
____

Sailing the Stars

AUTHOR'S PURPOSE
MONITOR AND FIX UP

SUMMARY This selection gives a brief history of space travel, beginning with the Cold War race to launch the first satellite in space and concluding in today's era of greater international cooperation. After following milestone developments such as the inclusion of women in the United States' and other countries' space programs, readers learn what it takes to be an astronaut, from science training to swimming tests.

LESSON VOCABULARY

accomplishments	focus
gravity	monitors
role	specific

INTRODUCE THE BOOK

INTRODUCE THE TITLE AND AUTHOR Discuss with students the title and author of *Sailing the Stars*. Draw students' attention to the Science content triangle. Ask: Does the title *Sailing the Stars* have a scientific ring to it? What images does the title create? Why do you think the author chose a poetic title for a scientific article?

BUILD BACKGROUND Invite students to discuss what they know about space travel, based on books, movies, museums, or other sources. Do you think the images you have of space travel are realistic? Encourage students to recall anything they've heard about *Sputnik*, Neil Armstrong, Sally Ride, or other people and events associated with space travel.

PREVIEW/USE TEXT FEATURES Have students take a few minutes to go over the Table of Contents, photos, captions, and boxes on pages 6 and 13 before reading the text. Ask: What do the photos add? Would illustrations have worked as well? Do photos seem more scientific? Why or why not? Can you guess from the text features whether the article is organized chronologically or geographically?

READ THE BOOK

SET PURPOSE Guide students to set their own purposes for reading the selection. Students' interest in space travel, astronomy, or other branches of science, or the history of pioneering women in science should guide this purpose. Invite them to use the pictures to come up with questions they would like to have answered, such as *What might it feel like to walk in space? How heavy are those suits? Why do astronauts learn to scuba dive? Could I become an astronaut?*

STRATEGY SUPPORT: MONITOR AND FIX UP
Encourage students to jot down any points that confuse them as they read. Suggest that they reread, read the surrounding text to understand context, or seek clarification from an outside source, such as a dictionary, the Internet, or a teacher.

COMPREHENSION QUESTIONS

PAGE 3 What can you tell about the author's purpose from the chapter titles? *(Possible response: She wants to inform readers about space travel.)*

PAGE 4 Notice that the definition for *orbit* is between commas in the sentence *A satellite is something that orbits, or travels around, a larger body in space.* Write a similarly constructed sentence that uses one of the vocabulary words. *(Responses will vary.)*

PAGE 11 What is one reason there were no women test pilots in the 1950s and 1960s? *(Possible response: Women were barred from the necessary training.)*

PAGE 17 What does the survival training tell you about the work of astronauts? *(Possible response: It is very dangerous.)*

REVISIT THE BOOK

READER RESPONSE

1. Possible response: To show that the U.S. and the U.S.S.R. were at odds. Their rivalry fueled the space program.
2. Responses will vary but should include the main points of the chapter.
3. screens; watches
4. Possible response: Please focus on your homework. The telescope was out of focus. Responses will vary for what information captions can provide.

EXTEND UNDERSTANDING Invite students to create their own graphic device that relates information from the article, such as a time line or a chart comparing the history of American and Russian space travel.

RESPONSE OPTIONS

WRITING Suggest that students imagine being the only woman or the only African American in a class of NASA astronauts. Ask them to write a paragraph or two describing their experience and feelings as pioneers in their field.

SCIENCE CONNECTION

TIME FOR Science

Have students research a pioneer in a field of their choosing, whether in science or the arts and humanities. Remind them that a pioneer is a person who breaks new ground. Ask them to share their research, including such details as what motivated or inspired the person.

Skill Work

TEACH/REVIEW VOCABULARY

Divide students into groups, give a time limit, and ask the groups to come up with as many synonyms as possible for each word. If synonyms prove difficult (such as for *gravity*), allow students to use phrases.

ELL Remind English language learners that words are often made of parts, such as *astro* and *naut* in *astronaut*. Encourage them to break the vocabulary words into their parts, using a dictionary if necessary.

TARGET SKILL AND STRATEGY

AUTHOR'S PURPOSE Tell students that an *author's purpose* is the reason or reasons that she or he has for writing (such as to persuade, inform, entertain, or express). Remind students they must often infer the author's purpose, based on text clues. *Sailing the Stars*, for example, contains dates, historic photos, and facts about the history of space travel. Ask: What does this suggest about the author's purpose? If the author's purpose in this selection were to entertain, would the selection be different?

MONITOR AND FIX UP Tell students that *monitoring* and *fixing up* is the process by which they keep track of their own comprehension. They should notice if the text stops making sense and ask such questions as *What does this mean? Why did the author include this?* Answering such questions will also help students identify the author's purpose.

ADDITIONAL SKILL INSTRUCTION

SEQUENCE Remind students that *sequence* is the order of events in a story or article. Point out that *Sailing the Stars* includes many dates. Help students see that the book is organized chronologically. Ask: What does ordering these events in this way tell you about the author's purpose? Suggest that students create their own time line of the events discussed in the article.

Name ____________________

Author's Purpose

- An **author's purpose** is the reason or reasons an author has for writing.
- Four common reasons are: **to persuade, to inform, to entertain, to express ideas.**

Directions Read the paragraphs below. Then answer the questions on the lines below.

In 2003, China joined an exclusive club when 38-year-old former fighter pilot Yang Liwei orbited Earth 14 times. China is now only the third country in history to have launched a person into space.

Space exploration is now a worldwide effort. Together we can learn new and exciting things. And, if you really try, perhaps you will be one of the people who sail the stars!

1. What would you say is the author's main purpose in writing the first paragraph?

____

2. Explain your answer.

____

____

3. What purpose might the author have in the second paragraph?

____

4. Explain your answer.

____

____

5. How do you think the author's two purposes might work together?

____

____

Name____

Vocabulary

Directions Choose the word from the box that best matches each definition. Write the word on the line.

Check the Words You Know

___accomplishments	___focus
___gravity	___monitors
___role	___specific

1. exact, definite ______________________
2. the force that pulls things towards Earth ______________________
3. computer screens that display data ______________________
4. to concentrate; an area of study or observation ______________________
5. a purpose or use of someone or something ______________________
6. successes, achievements; skills ______________________

Directions Write two sentences on the lines below about *Sailing the Stars*. Use as many vocabulary words as you can.

____

____

____

____

____

____

____

____

____

The Journey Through Earth

5.5.4

CAUSE AND EFFECT
SUMMARIZE

SUMMARY In this story, Mrs. Cieco's class learns about the layers of the Earth during a field trip to Mount Randall. Three students, Toby, Kenny, and Maria, travel through the Earth in a scientist's machine, experiencing Earth's layers first-hand.

LESSON VOCABULARY

armor	encases
extinct	hideous
plunged	serpent

INTRODUCE THE BOOK

INTRODUCE THE TITLE AND AUTHOR Discuss with students the title and the author of *The Journey Through Earth.* Based on the title, ask students to say what they think the book will be about. Ask students if they think this will be fiction or nonfiction and why.

BUILD BACKGROUND Discuss what students know about the layers of the Earth. Ask them how they think we know about the layers of the Earth. Ask them if they think it is possible to travel all the way through the Earth and to give reasons to support their point of view.

PREVIEW/USE TEXT FEATURES As students preview the book, have them notice the illustrations and chapter headings. Invite them to notice the diagram of Earth's layers on page 8.

READ THE BOOK

SET PURPOSE Have students set a purpose for reading *The Journey Through Earth.* Students' interest in what happens to Toby, Kenny, and Maria, as well as their interest in the layers of the Earth should guide this purpose. Suggest that students set two purposes: to find out what happens and to learn about Earth.

STRATEGY SUPPORT: SUMMARIZE As students read, suggest they *summarize* the plot in each chapter. Remind them that when you summarize, you write only about the most important ideas. You leave out less important details or ideas. Students may later want to put together their chapter summaries to create a summary of the selection.

COMPREHENSION QUESTIONS

PAGE 4 Why is it a special day? *(Toby's class is going on a field trip to Mount Randall.)*

PAGE 7 What are the five layers of the Earth? *(crust, upper mantle, mantle, outer core, inner core)*

PAGE 9 Why do the rock plates under the continents move? *(Heat in the mantle causes the huge rock plates under continents to move very slowly.)*

PAGE 10 What keeps the Earth's inner core solid? *(the weight of all the other layers creating pressure and the strength of its iron and nickel makeup)*

PAGE 13 What happened when Kenny and Toby climbed to the top of the volcano? *(They both slipped and fell to the bottom.)*

PAGE 21 What happened when Maria complained again about the heat? *(Kenny got the idea to tell the computer to make it cooler.)*

REVISIT THE BOOK

READER RESPONSE

1. The steering lever snapped and they couldn't turn the machine.
2. They began at Mount Randall near Seattle. They ended on Marion Island, a scientific research station just above Antarctica. They went through the crust, the upper mantle, mantle, outer core, and inner core. Possible responses: crust: increased heat; upper mantle: orange glow outside the craft; mantle: changing craft speeds; outer core: warning message not to continue; inner core: dull grey color outside the craft.
3. Possible response: A volcano becomes extinct when the geological action moves to a different location.
4. Responses will vary.

EXTEND UNDERSTANDING As students look at the illustration on page 28, ask them to say whether the plot in this story could really happen and why. Invite them to discuss what they can learn from this fictional story.

RESPONSE OPTIONS

WRITING Invite students to write a paragraph or two about cause-and-effect relationships in the story. They can use the chapter summaries they created earlier to help them. Encourage them to write about "why something happened" and "what happened." Have them use clue words such as *because, so,* and *since* to indicate relationships between why something happened and what happened.

SCIENCE CONNECTION

Students can learn more about the layers of Earth on the Internet or at the library. Suggest they learn more about Earth's inner core.

Skill Work

TEACH/REVIEW VOCABULARY

To reinforce the meaning of *extinct,* read the third paragraph on page 25. Ask students to say what they think *extinct* means, based on the context. What other words in the paragraph help them understand the meaning of *extinct?* Continue in a similar fashion with the remaining vocabulary words.

TARGET SKILL AND STRATEGY

CAUSE AND EFFECT Remind students that the *cause* is "why something happened." An *effect* is "what happened." Explain that clue words such as *because, so,* and *since* may indicate a cause-and-effect relationship. Suggest they track causes and effects as they read, using a graphic organizer.

ELL Help students use graphic organizers to list causes and effects involving things that happen in the classroom. Then have students read their organizers aloud, using clue words such as *because, so,* and *since* to indicate a relationship between why something happened and what happened.

SUMMARIZE Remind students that when you *summarize*, you make a brief statement that gives the main ideas of a story. As students read, suggest that they summarize a cause and an effect in each chapter.

ADDITIONAL SKILL INSTRUCTION

PLOT AND CHARACTER Remind students that the *plot* is the organized pattern of events in a story. Events usually happen in a sequence. Some events are more important than others. Remind them that a *character* is a person in a story. Authors usually describe their characters. They tell what they look like, how they act, and what kind of people they are. Invite students to track the plot of the selection. They may want to use a graphic organizer. Have them think about the characters in the story. Ask: What does the author tell about them?

Name ____________________

Cause and Effect

- A **cause** is "why something happened."
- An **effect** is "what happened."

Directions Draw a line to match each cause with its effect.

Cause	Effect
1. Convection cells in the Earth's mantle generate great heat.	Toby did not read the message to the others.
2. Toby and Kenny climb over the edge of the volcano.	The craft made the adjustments to get the power it needed.
3. The craft began to get too warm.	She discovered a hidden laboratory full of fossils.
4. Maria decided to have a closer look around the craft.	Toby asked the computer to make the craft cooler.
5. Minerals sink into a seashell, taking over the original cells.	A fossil is formed.
6. The computer message would scare Kenny and Maria.	They fall into the volcano.
7. The heat of the inner core pushed the machine to its limits.	Huge rock plates under the continents move slowly.

Directions Read the following sentence. Write an effect on the lines below.

Cause: The core of the Earth is too hot and deep for scientists to reach.

8. Effect: ____________________

____

____

Name ____

Vocabulary

Directions Write each word from the box next to its synonym.

Check the Words You Know

___armor ___encases ___extinct
___hideous ___plunged ___serpent

1. dead ____________________________
2. horrible ____________________________
3. snake ____________________________
4. encloses ____________________________
5. protective covering ____________________________
6. fell ____________________________

Directions Write a paragraph about *The Journey Through Earth*. Use as many vocabulary words as you can.

____

____

____

____

____

____

____

____

____

____

The United States Moves West

5.5.5

GENERALIZE
QUESTIONING

SUMMARY This reader outlines the westward expansion of the United States in the 1800s. It describes the search for resources that led to the Louisiana Purchase and Lewis and Clark's journey. It also describes the impact that this expansion had on the Native American peoples already living there.

LESSON VOCABULARY

- economic
- independence
- overrun
- scrawled
- vacant

INTRODUCE THE BOOK

INTRODUCE THE TITLE AND AUTHOR Introduce students to the title and author of the book *The United States Moves West*. Based on the title, ask students what kind of information they think this book will provide. Ask students if they are familiar with any of the men pictured on the front cover.

BUILD BACKGROUND Ask students if they know anything about Lewis and Clark's expedition. What are some of the states they traveled through? What ocean did they finally reach?

PREVIEW/USE TEXT FEATURES Suggest students skim the text and look at the illustrations, maps, and captions. Ask students what they think the text will be about.

READ THE BOOK

SET PURPOSE Have students set a purpose for reading *The United States Moves West*. Students' interest and curiosity about exploration and American history can guide this purpose.

STRATEGY SUPPORT: QUESTIONING Remind students that expert readers ask questions as they read. This helps them test their comprehension and lets them know what answers to look for as they read. Encourage students to write down questions on sticky notes and place them on the page. When they are finished reading, they can return to the page to see if they can answer the question.

COMPREHENSION QUESTIONS

PAGE 6 Whom did Jefferson send to Paris to try to buy New Orleans? *(James Monroe)*

PAGE 7 Which country owned Louisiana at the time just before the Purchase? *(France)*

PAGE 12 Which river did Lewis and Clark start out on? *(Missouri River)*

PAGE 16 What mountain range did Lewis and Clark run into? *(the Rocky Mountains)*

PAGE 22 As a result of the United States western expansion, where did Native American groups end up living? *(on reservations)*

REVISIT THE BOOK

READER RESPONSE

1. Possible responses: Generalization—Early trips to the west were long and difficult journeys. Details—Explorers needed help from tribes they met; explorers had to trade horses and food with tribes; explorers had to cross difficult terrain such as the Rocky Mountains.
2. Responses will vary.
3. *Co* means *together*; when you add this to *exist*, you get a word that means *to live together.*
   Possible responses for additional words: co-worker, co-pilot.
   Sentences will vary.
4. Responses will vary.

EXTEND UNDERSTANDING Study the book together with the students and discuss how the inset photographs add to or take away from the historical photos.

RESPONSE OPTIONS

WRITING Have the students write a letter from the point of view of Meriwether Lewis or one of his fellow explorers. They are spending their winter in Oregon, having finally reached the Pacific Ocean. This letter is to be sent home, telling their families about their adventures finding the passage to the west.

SOCIAL STUDIES CONNECTION

Time For SOCIAL STUDIES

Have students research Lewis and Clark's expedition using the Internet or the library. Have them go into detail about one aspect of the journey, such as the winter in Oregon, the size of the crew, or some of the Native American tribes they met.

Skill Work

TEACH/REVIEW VOCABULARY

To reinforce the contextual meaning of the word *vacant* on page 20, discuss with students the words leading up to it: "Settlers began moving into the area, but this land was not *vacant*." Do the words around it help give clues as to the meaning of *vacant*? Continue with the other vocabulary words

ELL Write the vocabulary words on cards. Distribute the cards to students. Challenge students to go on a scavenger hunt to find other books, magazines, or newspapers containing the same words.

TARGET SKILL AND STRATEGY

GENERALIZE Because this book presents a number of results of westward expansion, students will need to organize these facts to *generalize*. As they read, have them consider what the main outcomes of Lewis and Clark's expedition were.

QUESTIONING Remind students that both *asking questions* and *answering questions* can help them better understand the text. Encourage students to use text features such as headings, pictures, and captions to help them pose questions. Point out that as they read, they can use information in the text and prior knowledge to answer their questions.

ADDITIONAL SKILL INSTRUCTION

FACT AND OPINION Remind students that a statement of *fact* is a statement that can be proven to be true, and that a statement of *opinion* can be true or not true. To give students practice, give them several sentences, some of which are fact and some opinion, and have them mark them as such. Then have students write their own statements of fact and statements of opinion about any topic they choose.

Name ________________________________

Generalize

- A **generalization** is a broad statement or rule that applies to many examples. A generalization is made after thinking about a number of examples or facts and what they have in common.
- A **valid generalization** is adequately supported by specific facts and logic.
- A **faulty generalization** is not adequately supported by facts or logic.

Directions Review *The United States Moves West.* Write whether each generalization below is *valid* or *faulty.*

1. ______________ Around 1800, some Americans feared that France would block their movement westward.

2. ______________ All Americans supported the Louisiana Purchase.

3. ______________ On their expedition, Lewis and Clark made friendly contact with many Native Americans in the West.

4. ______________ Every conflict between the settlers and local tribes had to be settled by the U.S. government.

5. ______________ Many people hoped that the tribes and settlers would coexist peacefully.

6. ______________ Before the early 1800s, no President took an interest in the lands to the west.

7. ______________ Lewis and Clark had to overcome many obstacles as they traveled west to the Pacific Ocean.

8. ______________ In the early 1800s, few tribes were forced off their lands.

9. ______________ The U.S. government always honored its treaties with Native American tribes.

Name____

Vocabulary

Directions Choose the word from the box that best completes each sentence.

Check the Words You Know

___economic
___independence
___vacant
___overrun
___scrawled

1. Lewis quickly _______________ an entry in his journal describing the encounter he had that day with members of the Oto tribe.
2. The _______________ land that had been set aside for Native American tribes grew smaller and smaller.
3. After the British colonies won their _______________ , the interest in expanding west became stronger.
4. One _______________ reason for wanting to expand west was trade.
5. The settlement was soon _______________ with soldiers.

Directions Write a brief paragraph discussing Lewis and Clark's journey west, using at least four of the vocabulary words.

____

____

____

____

____

____

Driven to Change

DRAW CONCLUSIONS
IMPORTANT IDEAS

SUMMARY In this nonfiction selection, the idea of changing the way students get to and from school is explored. Four schools across the United States have already made big changes in getting students to walk or bike instead of driving or riding the bus. These changes are big efforts to help reduce the use of fossil fuels and, therefore, help save Earth. These changes are also helping students improve their health through daily exercise.

LESSON VOCABULARY

bizarre	breathtaking	headline
high-pitched	roost	vital

INTRODUCE THE BOOK

INTRODUCE THE TITLE AND AUTHOR Discuss the title and author of *Driven to Change*. Discuss what is happening in the cover photograph. Ask: What kind of "driving" is occurring in this photograph? What could these bikers be "changing?"

BUILD BACKGROUND Discuss how students currently get to school. Ask them if they think the way they are getting to school is helping Earth and their health. If not, ask: What changes could you make to help Earth and your health? Discuss how students get to other places such as a friend's house or sports practice and what changes they can make to better help Earth and their health.

PREVIEW/USE TEXT FEATURES After students have previewed the book, discuss the various features such as Table of Contents, photographs, captions, chapters, headings, charts, and Glossary. Have students turn to pages 18–19. Explain the usefulness of these charts. Point out that the bullet points are used to organize information in a way so that the reader can get it quickly.

READ THE BOOK

SET PURPOSE Have students set a purpose for reading *Driven to Change*. Ask them to think about and list the ways they have seen fellow students get to their school.

STRATEGY SUPPORT: IMPORTANT IDEAS Have students turn to page 3. Remind students that a Table of Contents provides the overall important ideas in a book and that the details given in the text of the chapters support those ideas.

COMPREHENSION QUESTIONS

PAGE 4 Why do you think the author included information by percentages? *(Possible response: To inform with facts that show undeniable impact on health and the environment)*

PAGES 6–7 What conclusion can you make about urban sprawl? *(Responses may vary but make sure students understand the concept of drawing conclusions and the meaning of urban sprawl.)*

PAGES 10–15 What is the common important idea among these four schools? *(Possible response: Healthier ways to get to school.)*

PAGE 19 Why do you think the author states, "Science Says . . ."? *(Possible response: To support these facts through research.)*

REVISIT THE BOOK

READER RESPONSE

1. Possible responses: Columbia, MO: Walking School Bus; Duluth, GA: Bike Train; Gadsden, AL: Driving Protest. Responses may vary but make sure students understand the concept of drawing conclusions.
2. Responses may vary but make sure students understand the concept of important ideas.
3. Responses may vary but make sure students understand the meaning of *vital.*
4. Responses may vary but make sure students understand the meaning of *effects*.

EXTEND UNDERSTANDING Using the information on pages 20–23, discuss what Global Warming means and its effects on Earth. Discuss the positive benefits for Earth from making changes of how people get from one place to another.

ELL To check students' understanding, have them use the photographs on pages 22–23 to retell about some of the effects of Global Warming.

RESPONSE OPTIONS

LANGUAGE ARTS As a class, have students create a survey of how people get to school. Next, have students in the class (and, if possible, throughout the school) complete the survey. Then, have students tally the results and chart the findings. Have each student write a conclusion about the results and then share with the class.

SOCIAL STUDIES CONNECTION

Have students develop a plan to encourage others to take a "healthier route" to school. Students can create posters, fliers, and awards to promote their plan. With approval from the school's administration, help students implement the plan and drive change at your school.

Skill Work

TEACH/REVIEW VOCABULARY

Have students locate the vocabulary words within the text and use context clues to write a definition for each word. Student can use the Glossary to check their definitions. Then have students write a sentence for each word.

TARGET SKILL AND STRATEGY

DRAW CONCLUSIONS Remind students that a *conclusion* is a sensible decision reached after thinking about details or facts in what is read. Read page 4 with students. Ask them what conclusion can be drawn about the study results regarding students riding the bus or being driven to school versus walking or biking. *(In 2004, 37 percent more students rode the bus or drove to school than in 1999.)* As students read, have them write conclusions and list the details or facts that support their conclusions.

IMPORTANT IDEAS Remind students that *important ideas* are the major parts or topics of a story, and that important ideas are often presented in nonfiction texts through various types of graphic features. Explain that each important idea is supported by details. Have students turn to page 19. Discuss the important ideas stated at each bullet point and the details given in the text below each bulleted idea.

ADDITIONAL SKILL INSTRUCTION

AUTHOR'S PURPOSE Remind students that authors often write to inform, persuade, express, or entertain. Ask: Why do you think Becky Cheston wrote *Driven to Change*? What in the text makes you think that is the purpose? Have students share their idea of the purpose and examples from the text that support that purpose.

Name ____________________________________

Draw Conclusions

- **Drawing Conclusions** means to make sensible decisions after thinking about details or facts in what you read.

Directions Below are four conclusions from *Driven to Change*. Go back to the book and find supporting details for each conclusion.

1. **Conclusion:** Urban sprawl has caused many problems.

   Supporting details: ____________________________________

   ____

   ____

2. **Conclusion:** School communities have found creative ways to get students to school without driving.

   Supporting details: ____________________________________

   ____

   ____

3. **Conclusion:** Exercise is beneficial.

   Supporting details: ____________________________________

   ____

   ____

4. **Conclusion:** Driving less will help our planet.

   Supporting details: ____________________________________

   ____

   ____

Name ______________________________

Vocabulary

Directions Write the word from the box that best matches each clue.

Check the Words You Know

___bizarre	___breathtaking	___headline
___high-pitched	___roost	___vital

1. The newspaper puts this at the top of each article. ____________
2. It is a place to stay. ____________
3. This is something very strange. ____________
4. This sound could break glass. ____________
5. It is very important. ____________
6. The beauty is so incredible! ____________

Directions Write a paragraph using all of the vocabulary words.

____
____
____
____
____
____
____
____
____
____
____
____

The Kudzu Invasion

MAIN IDEA AND DETAILS
TEXT STRUCTURE

SUMMARY This book discusses the kudzu plant's introduction to America. The kudzu plant grew so rapidly that it took over a large amount of land, ruining crops and even pulling down farmhouses. It was almost impossible to kill. It also had benefits, like serving as a healthy food for animals.

LESSON VOCABULARY

bleached	carcasses
decay	parasites
scrawny	starvation
suspicions	tundra

INTRODUCE THE BOOK

INTRODUCE THE TITLE AND AUTHOR Discuss with students the title and the author of *The Kudzu Invasion.* Based on the title and cover photograph, ask students what they think this book will tell them about the kudzu plant. Ask how the title is a clue to the book's contents.

BUILD BACKGROUND Ask students to describe ecosystems with which they are familiar, like deserts, rain forests, or the tundra. Then ask them to name various plants that live in each ecosystem. For example, cacti live in the desert. Prompt them to think about their own environment and ask them what plants they see around their home or school.

PREVIEW/USE TEXT FEATURES As students preview the book, ask them to look at the photographs and captions. Have them look at the photograph on page 12 and ask them what they think the author will tell them about the kudzu plant.

READ THE BOOK

SET PURPOSE Have students set a purpose for reading *The Kudzu Invasion.* Students' interest in strange plants should guide this purpose. Suggest that students think about how plants can effect our environment.

STRATEGY SUPPORT: TEXT STRUCTURE As students read, recognizing a text's structure or organization of ideas will help them with comprehension. A graphic organizer can help students keep track of the important ideas in a text. Using a compare-and-contrast graphic organizer, ask students to list the effects the kudzu plant has on its environment.

COMPREHENSION QUESTIONS

PAGE 6 What is the main idea of the first paragraph on this page? *(The kudzu plant has benefits.)*

PAGE 6 What details support the main idea of the first paragraph on this page? *(It can prevent erosion because it has long roots that grip the soil. It contains protein and vitamins that make it a good food source for cattle.)*

PAGE 10 What effects has the kudzu plant had on plants and animals in the forest habitat? *(It has taken over forests, causing plants and animals to die.)*

PAGES 14–17 If you were a southern farmer, which way would you choose to destroy kudzu on your farm? Why? *(Answers will vary, but students should support their answer with a solid reason.)*

REVISIT THE BOOK

READER RESPONSE

1. Detail: Kudzu's long roots grip the soil and prevent erosion.
   Detail: Kudzu provides nourishing feed for livestock.
   Detail: In the 1930s, the U.S. government paid farmers to plant kudzu.
   Main Idea: In the early 1900s, kudzu was considered beneficial and valuable.
2. I. Introduction of kudzu to the United States
   II. Benefits of kudzu
   III. Hazards of kudzu
   IV. Controlling kudzu
   V. Uses for kudzu
   Answers about author's view will vary. Students should give a viable explanation.
3. *hab;* definition: to have, hold, or dwell; two other words: *inhabit, habitation*
4. Answers will vary. Students should support their answers.

EXTEND UNDERSTANDING As students look at the photographs, ask them why certain ones help them understand what the author is saying. Ask them to point to specific photographs to help them explain their ideas. Draw their attention to the photographs on pages 8 and 11. Ask students to discuss how these photographs help illustrate the kudzu's negative effects on an environment.

RESPONSE OPTIONS

WRITING Ask students to think about ways that plants affect our environment. Prompt them to think about the benefits and problems that plants have. Ask them to use a graphic organizer and list the benefits and problems of the kudzu plant or another plant that they have studied.

SCIENCE CONNECTION

TIME FOR Science

Students can learn more about the kudzu plant or other plants that interest them by researching it on the Internet or in the library. Suggest that they find another invasive plant like the kudzu and compare the two.

Skill Work

TEACH/REVIEW VOCABULARY

Have students look up each vocabulary word in a dictionary and write a short definition for each word. Then have them use each word in a sentence. Have volunteers share their sentences with the class.

ELL Have students look up the meaning of each vocabulary word. Then have them write a translation for each word in their home language.

TARGET SKILL AND STRATEGY

MAIN IDEA AND DETAILS Remind students that the *main idea* is the most important idea about a topic. Supporting *details* are small pieces of information that tell more about the main idea. Using a graphic organizer, have students write the main idea and supporting details of each section as they read.

TEXT STRUCTURE Reinforce to students that recognizing *text structure* is the ability to recognize the organization of a piece of writing. As students read *The Kudzu Invasion,* have them answer questions in a graphic organizer with the headings *Problems* and *Solutions.* What is the problem? Who is trying to solve the problem? How did that person or persons try to solve the problem? What are the results of these solutions? Is the problem solved? Why or why not?

ADDITIONAL SKILL INSTRUCTION

GENERALIZE Remind students that sometimes when they read, they are given ideas about several things or people and they can make a statement about all of them together. This statement is called a *generalization.* Valid generalizations are accurate or true. Tell them that clue words, such as *most, all, always,* and *never* can help them identify generalizations in what they read. As students read, have them make generalizations about people's attitudes toward the kudzu. Ask them to list facts to support their generalizations.

Name ______________________________

Main Idea and Details

- The **main idea** is the most important idea about a topic.
- Supporting **details** are small pieces of information that tell more about the main ideas.

Directions Read the following two paragraphs. Then use the diagrams below to write the main idea and supporting details of each paragraph.

Bringing plants from one country to another is not always a good thing. The exotic plant may grow so fast that it crowds out local plant life. The kudzu has been doing this in the South. It has found a habitat without insects or frost to kill it. During the summer, kudzu can grow as much as a foot a day.

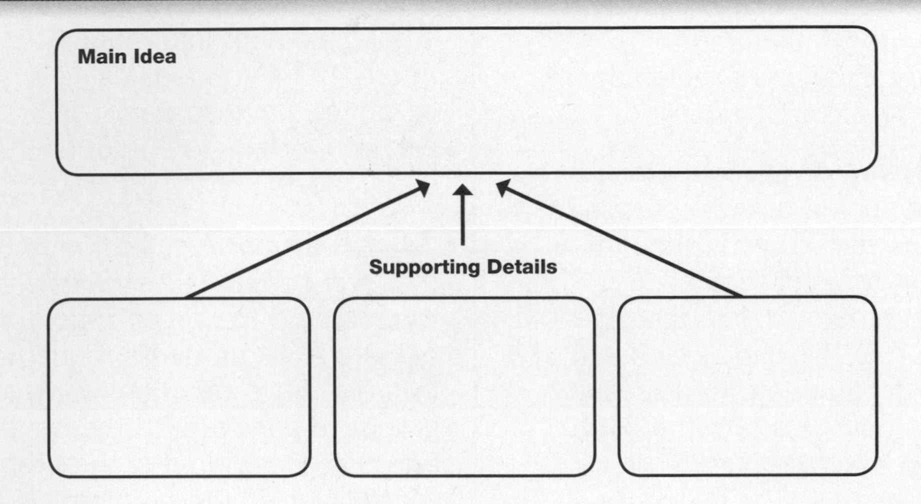

Kudzu even attacks human-made structures. Eventually, the vines that Channing Cope planted pulled down his farmhouse. Today, farmers are forever trying to protect their houses and barns from the killer plant. It is strong enough to destroy power lines too. Power and telephone companies spend a lot of money to repair the lines that the kudzu has damaged.

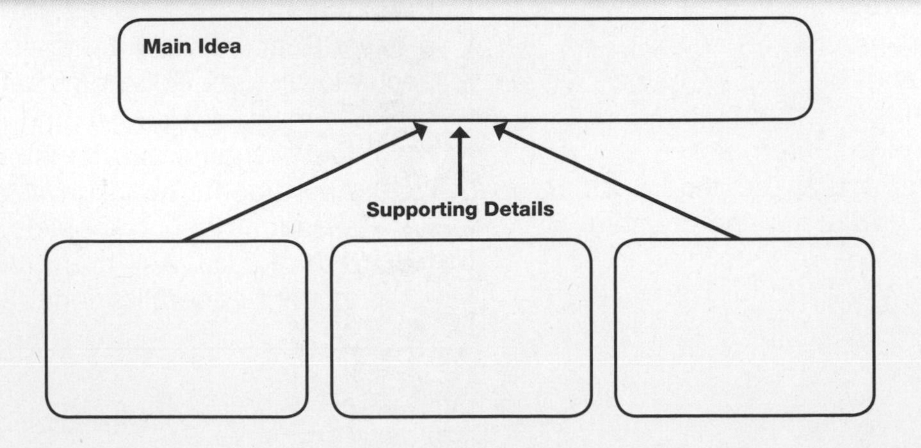

Name ____

Vocabulary

Directions Write the vocabulary word that matches each underlined word or phrase.

Check the Words You Know

___bleached	___carcasses	___decay	___parasites
___scrawny	___starvation	___suspicions	___tundra

1. If plants don't get enough sun they fade to a whitish green. ______________________
2. It was a biologist who first had doubts about the plant. ______________________
3. The flowers did not have any water and they were in a state of ruin. ______________________
4. The biologist examined the remains of the dead trees. ______________________
5. The kudzu forced the other plants to go on a bread and water diet. ______________________
6. The tree was dying because freeloaders were attaching to its leaves. ______________________
7. On a walk through the forest, the biologist noticed rotting matter under the fallen leaves.

   ____
8. The thin plant was much smaller than the rest. ______________________
9. There was a treeless area of frozen earth where nothing grew. ______________________
10. If your doubts are correct, then I would not plant the tree so close to the house.

    ____

Directions Write one sentence that contains two of the words from the box.

____

____

____

____

____

The Golden Journey

COMPARE AND CONTRAST
STORY STRUCTURE

SUMMARY This story follows the members of a family as they leave their farm and join other gold diggers on the California Trail heading off in search of a new life in the West. After surviving the long trek, many hardships, and the disappointment of finding very few nuggets in several mining towns, the family finally settles in San Francisco, where Pa starts a successful construction business.

LESSON VOCABULARY

adorn	cleanse
lifeless	precious
realm	spoonful

INTRODUCE THE BOOK

INTRODUCE THE TITLE AND AUTHOR Discuss with students the title and author of *The Golden Journey*. Draw students' attention to the cover art, and have them describe what they can tell about the story based on the picture.

BUILD BACKGROUND Invite students to discuss what they know about the California Gold Rush. Locate Missouri, the Sierra Nevada, and San Francisco on a map. Ask: Have you ever moved with your family from one home to another? How far away did you move? What was it like moving to a new home?

PREVIEW Go over the Table of Contents on page 3. Explain that the book is about a family that travels by covered wagon across the western United States in 1849. Point out that the chapter headings suggest that the story will be chronologically organized. Then have students skim through the illustrations and boxed diary entries in the book. Ask them to use these to predict what may have happened on this trip and what happens at the end of the story.

READ THE BOOK

SET PURPOSE Guide students to set their own purposes for reading the selection. Have them look through the book again and use the pictures to create questions they would like to have answered, such as "What kinds of items did families put inside covered wagons? Were the wagons warm at night?"

STRATEGY SUPPORT: STORY STRUCTURE Remind students that every story has a beginning, middle, and end. This makes up the structure of the story. In *The Golden Journey*, the author further organized the text by separating sections into chapters. Have students preview the chapter titles and use them to make predictions about the story's plot.

COMPREHENSION QUESTIONS

PAGES 5–6 How was Josh's response to the news of the family's move similar to Susannah's response? How was it different? *(Both had to leave some items behind. Susannah cried, while Josh looked forward to the trip.)*

PAGE 11 Why was Susannah more bored than Josh during the trip? *(She had no one her own age to play with.)*

PAGE 19 How did the families help each other cross the Sierra Nevada? *(They used all the oxen they owned to haul one wagon at a time up the mountain.)*

PAGE 22 Pa had a smile on his face after learning that Pleasant Valley had been mined out, but Weaverville still had gold. What does that reveal about his character? *(He was patient and optimistic.)*

REVISIT THE BOOK

READER RESPONSE

1. Possible response: Weaverville: Josh worked alongside the adults, didn't go to school, and had no friends
   San Francisco: he went to school and played with friends
   Both places: Josh had responsibilities
2. Possible response: Each chapter title gave a clue about what that section would be about.
3. Paragraphs will vary.
4. Possible response: people who dreamed of a better life and had the patience and endurance to withstand hardship and change

EXTEND UNDERSTANDING Explain to students that fictional stories often have themes, or big ideas, that convey a general truth or opinion. Remind students that themes are often implied in fiction, rather than stated directly. Help students find the theme of *The Golden Journey*, such as, "Patience, hard work, and optimism allow people to overcome challenges." Encourage students to use their own words to state the theme in a way that makes sense to them.

RESPONSE OPTIONS

WRITING Suggest that students imagine crossing the plains long ago in a covered wagon. Have them write a brief description of one day during the trip, including what they might do and anything they might notice about the landscape or wildlife.

MUSIC CONNECTION

Have students write the words to a song similar to the campfire song on page 9. Ask whether they know any traditional American songs. Invite students to get ideas for their own lyrics and melodies by using the Internet or asking older family members or neighbors if they know any historic folk songs. Invite volunteers to share their songs.

Skill Work

TEACH/REVIEW VOCABULARY

Have students come up with a related word, synonym, or antonym for each vocabulary word. Ask other students to guess the vocabulary word associated with the new word. Then have students identify whether the new word is a related word, synonym, or antonym.

ELL Students can compare the English terminology used to describe the trek across the plains (such as *buffalo, wagon, hail,* or *smoke*) with translations of those words in their home language.

TARGET SKILL AND STRATEGY

COMPARE AND CONTRAST Remind students that to *compare* is to identify how two or more things are alike and to *contrast* is to identify how they are different. As students read through this book, have them look for similarities and differences between life on the California Trail, life in a mining camp, and life in San Francisco. Suggest they make a chart to keep track of similarities and differences.

STORY STRUCTURE Review with students that *story structure* is the way the author organizes the story. Have students create a story sequence chart. After reading *The Golden Journey*, have them fill out the chart with what happened in the beginning, middle, and end of the story.

ADDITIONAL SKILL INSTRUCTION

CHARACTER Review with students that a *character* is a person or animal who takes part in the events of a story. Suggest that students look for clues about what characters are like in this story. What does Josh do with the first gold nugget he finds, for example? What does that say about his character? What do people in the story say about Josh and what does that reveal? How does Pa react to the disappointment of finding very little gold? What does Ma's reaction to burning her favorite chair say about her character?

Name ____________________________________

Compare and Contrast

- To **compare** is to tell how two or more things are alike. Authors may use clue words and phrases such as *similar to, like,* or *as*.
- To **contrast** is to tell how two or more things are different. Authors may use clue words such as *different from, but, unlike, on the other hand,* or *however* to contrast.

Directions Read the two passages below. Compare and contrast the crises described and the way in which the characters confronted and overcame them. Then fill in the Venn Diagram below.

The river was swollen and raging. "It's because of that darned storm," one man said. But the men decided to go forward. One by one, the wagons slowly made their way across the river, the women and children in the back of the wagons and the men sitting up front. One by one, the families gathered and watched the people still to come. Finally, as the last wagon, with a hog tied to its back, was making the crossing, a gush of water came down the river. The hog disappeared. Only a piece of rope was left. When the wagon finally made it to solid land, a woman looked like she was about to cry. Her husband put his arm around her shoulders. "At least it was only the pig," he said.

As they climbed higher into the mountains, it got much colder. The campfires burned only dimly, hardly able to chase away the cold air. Susannah shivered while she slept. The next night, Ma pulled Pa aside. In an instant, Pa chopped up Ma's favorite chair and threw it on the fire. The blaze shot up and Susannah and Joshua inched closer to the flame. Joshua looked at his mother as she watched a piece of her family history go up in smoke. She didn't look sad, just determined.

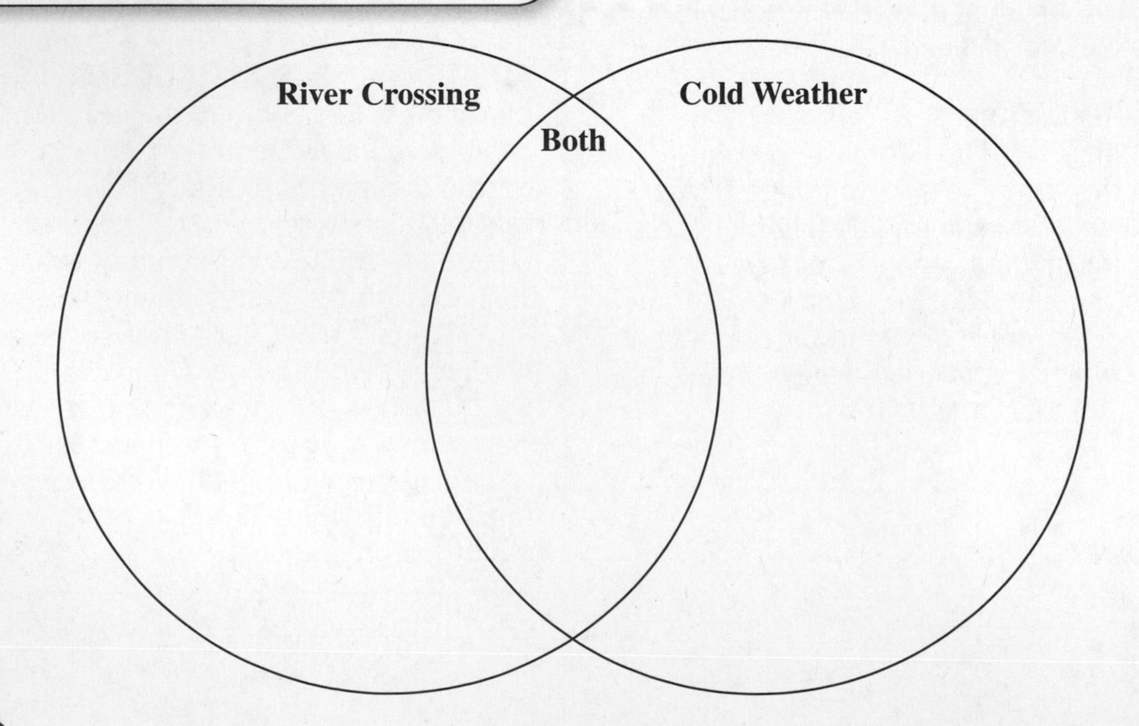

Name ______________________________

Vocabulary

Directions Choose a word from the box that best completes each sentence.

Check the Words You Know

___adorn	___cleanse	___lifeless
___precious	___realm	___spoonful

1. Mark added a ____________________ of honey to his tea.
2. A diamond is more ____________________ than a trinket.
3. The king was ruler of his ____________________.
4. Chemical scrubbers can ____________________ polluted air.
5. To dress up for the party, ____________________ yourself with ribbons and bows.
6. The animal's ____________________ body was on the ground.

Directions Read each group of words and circle the word that does not belong.

7.	a. kingdom	b. region	c. ruler	d. realm
8.	a. inert	b. lifeless	c. energetic	d. still
9.	a. valuable	b. generous	c. priceless	d. precious
10.	a. dismantle	b. decorate	c. adorn	d. embellish

Directions Write a short paragraph about the California Gold Rush. Use at least three words from the box.

____

____

____

____

____

Stop That Train!

FACT AND OPINION
PREDICT AND SET PURPOSE

SUMMARY *Stop That Train!* recounts the dangers involved in the early years of American train travel. This nonfiction reader provides information on some famous railroad accidents of the 1800s and how improvements in technology have made train travel safer.

LESSON VOCABULARY

criticizing	cruised	drenching
era	explosion	hydrogen

INTRODUCE THE BOOK

INTRODUCE THE TITLE AND AUTHOR Discuss with students the title and the author of *Stop That Train!* Based on the title, cover photograph, genre, and content triangle, ask students what they expect this book to be about. *(Possible response: the history of famous trains)*

BUILD BACKGROUND Discuss the advantages of train travel over car, bus, or truck travel. Point out to students that some of these aspects of train travel that people take for granted today were not at all common in the early days of railroads. Explain that train travel in the 1800s came with some danger, as the selection they are about to read will show.

ELL Invite students to tell about train trips they have taken, whether aboard large passenger trains or smaller commuter trains. Discuss the use of trains for transporting goods as well as people.

PREVIEW/USE TEXT FEATURES Have students skim through the book, focusing on the pictures and the maps. Ask students what differences they see between the trains in the pictures and the trains of today *(older engines, smoke coming out of smokestacks)*. Draw students' attention to the map on page 3, and talk about how this map from the 1800s looks different from modern maps of the United States.

READ THE BOOK

SET PURPOSE Have students think about the title of the book and set their own purpose for reading based on the title and subject of the selection.

STRATEGY SUPPORT: PREDICT AND SET PURPOSE Help students determine the meaning of *predict*. (to tell what you think might happen next in the story or article based on what has already happened) Read the first page aloud and then ask students to predict what will happen when railroads are developed. Have students give reasons for their predictions. Ask: What clues on the page helped you make your prediction? Tell students that as they continue to read, they are reading for the purpose of confirming or revising their predictions.

COMPREHENSION QUESTIONS

PAGE 5 Name one opinion found on this page. How do you know it's the author's opinion? *(You'd imagine that everyone would want to ride the new trains. I cannot check in a reference book to find out what everyone thought.)*

PAGE 10 Give an example of a generalization that the author makes. *(Possible response: Most of the time the brakemen did not pull the lever at the exact same time.)*

PAGE 17 What question do you have after reading this page? Where could you look for an answer? *(Possible response: Why was the prime meridian set to run through Greenwich, England? I could look in an encyclopedia.)*

PAGE 18 Look at the sentence, "Jones died in a heroic effort to stop his train." Is this a fact or an opinion? Explain your answer. *(Opinion; Although Jones's death might be a fact, it's the author's opinion that his death was heroic.)*

REVISIT THE BOOK

READER RESPONSE

1. Possible responses: FACTS: 1.) In 1804, the first steam-powered locomotive came on the scene. 2.) By 1840, there were already more than 2,800 miles of railway stretching across nine states. 3.) On May 10, 1869, the railroads met in Promontory Point, Utah. All three statements can be checked and proved true or false. OPINIONS: 1.) Most people were very excited about this new way of getting from place to place. 2.) You risked death to ride a train. 3.) Trains will always be an important part of our history. These statements tell of one person's ideas or feelings; they cannot be checked.
2. Responses will vary.
3. *cruised:* to travel without destination or purpose; to move smoothly or effortlessly
4. Responses will vary.

EXTEND UNDERSTANDING Point out that sometimes authors use graphic sources, such as maps, time lines, and photographs with captions, to provide additional information. Have students reread pages 8 and 9. Ask: What question do you have after reading these pages? How does the map on page 9 help you answer the question?

RESPONSE OPTIONS

SPEAKING AND WRITING Provide students with a copy of the ballad "Casey Jones." Have volunteers read the lyrics aloud. Then have students write a paragraph summarizing the Casey Jones song, describing some of the facts and opinions in it.

SOCIAL STUDIES CONNECTION

Time For SOCIAL STUDIES

Have students research what it was like to work on the railroads in the 1800s. Assign related topics to groups, such as living and working conditions for railroad workers or tactics used by railroad companies to recruit workers. Have groups prepare reports on their topics and share them with the class.

Skill Work

TEACH/REVIEW VOCABULARY

Pair students, and have each student in the pair write sentences for the vocabulary words, leaving a blank in place of the vocabulary word in each sentence. Have partners try to complete each other's sentences without using the glossary.

TARGET SKILL AND STRATEGY

FACT AND OPINION Remind students that a *fact* is a statement that can be proved true or false. An *opinion* is a statement of a person's ideas or beliefs. Emphasize that a fact may be true *or* false, but it is different from an opinion in that it can be checked. Give an example of a fact from the book and how it can be checked. Also provide an example of an opinion and discuss with students why the statement is an opinion. Have students read the book looking for statements of fact and opinion that the author makes.

PREDICT AND SET PURPOSE Remind students that to *predict* means to tell what might happen in a story based in what has already been read. Invite students to choose places as they read to stop and write their predictions of what might happen next in the text. Have them then read for the purpose of confirming or revising these predictions.

ADDITIONAL SKILL INSTRUCTION

GENERALIZE Review with students that when they *generalize,* they are making a general statement that applies to many facts or ideas in a passage or book. Point out that generalizations can show how ideas are all or mostly the same or different. Remind students of the clue words that signal generalizations, such as *usually, always, most, never, few.* Have students look for one generalization that the author makes and make one generalization of their own about early train travel.

Name ______________________________

Fact and Opinion

- A **statement of fact** is a statement that can be proved true or false. Even if it is false, it is a statement of fact that is incorrect.
- A **statement of opinion** tells a person's ideas or feelings. It cannot be proved true or false.

Some sentences contain both facts and opinions.

Directions Read each sentence from *Stop That Train!* Tell whether it is a statement of fact or of opinion and explain your answer.

1. Trains will always be an important part of our history—and the stories of the brave people who died building and driving them will continue to inspire us.

____

____

2. Casey Jones is the most famous engineer to die in a train wreck.

____

____

3. Today, air brakes are used in trains, buses, streetcars, and even planes in flight.

____

____

Directions Answer the following questions.

4. How many pages is *Train Wreck!*? What is the topic of this book?

____

____

____

5. Would you recommend this book? Why or why not?

____

____

____

Name ________________________________

Vocabulary

Directions Write the word from the box that belongs in each group.

Check the Words You Know

___criticizing	___cruised	___drenching
___era	___explosion	___hydrogen

1. moved, traveled, ______________________

2. pouring, soaking, ______________________

3. oxygen, helium, ______________________

4. period, time, ______________________

5. blast, bang, ______________________

6. finding fault, ______________________

Directions The base word of *criticizing* is *critic*. Look up the word *critic* in the dictionary. Write the definition at the center of the word web below. Then fill in the surrounding ovals on the web with other words that have *critic* as their base. Write the definitions of these words too.

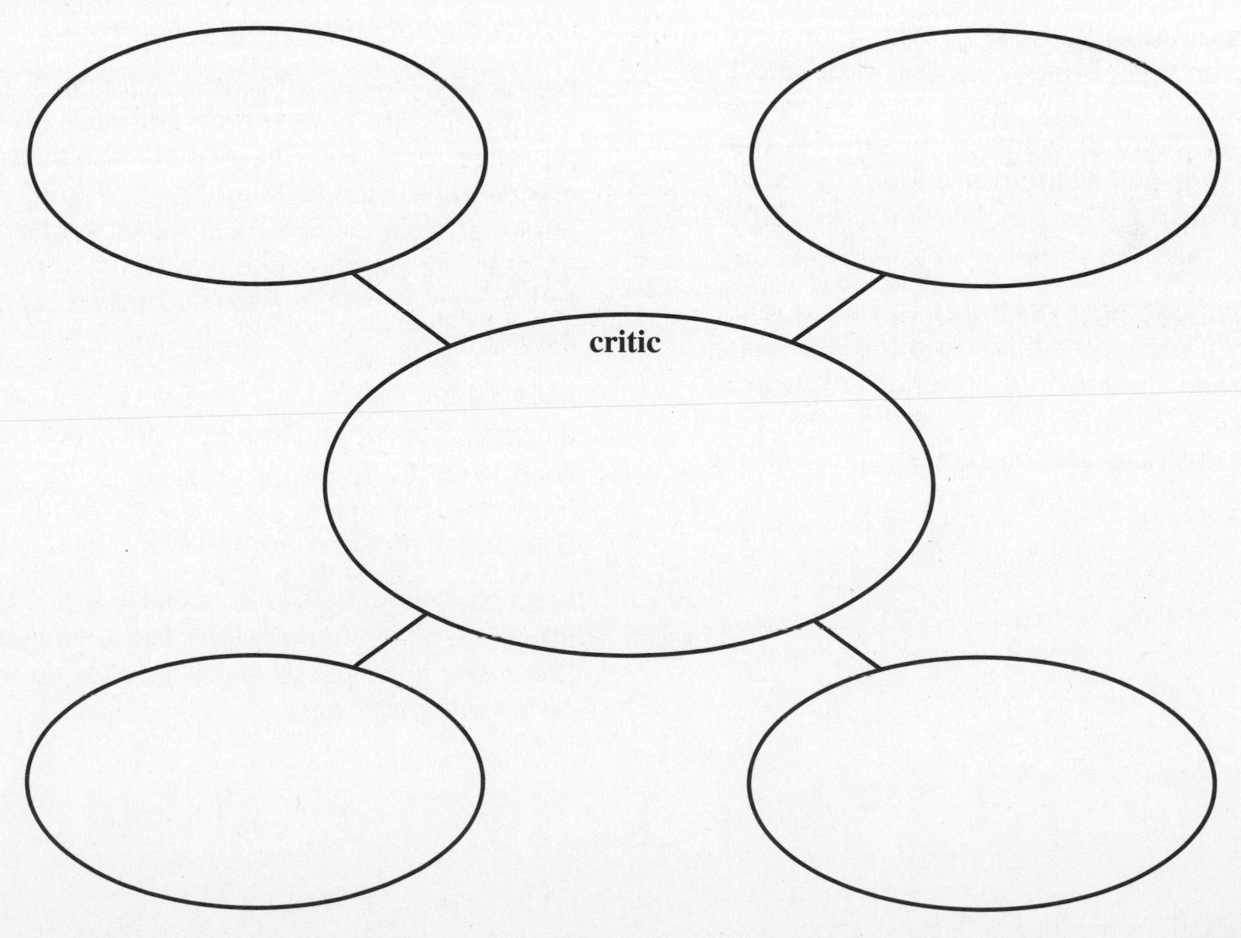

Grandma Betty's Banjo

SEQUENCE
PRIOR KNOWLEDGE

SUMMARY The author uses flashbacks to draw a comparison between a grandmother and granddaughter's interest in music. Students draw upon their prior knowledge of music and family relationships as they read about the positive effects of music and role models.

LESSON VOCABULARY

bass	clarinet
fidgety	forgetful
jammed	nighttime
secondhand	

INTRODUCE THE BOOK

INTRODUCE THE TITLE AND AUTHOR Discuss with students the title and author of *Grandma Betty's Banjo*. Encourage students to comment on how the illustration on the cover relates to the title. Ask students if the book is fiction or nonfiction.

BUILD BACKGROUND Arrange with your librarian to play an Elvis Presley recording or video for the class. Encourage class discussion about students' favorite types of music. Ask the students if any of them are learning to play an instrument. Discuss how different types of music make them feel.

PREVIEW/USE TEXT FEATURES Have students look at the chapter titles and the illustrations. Encourage students to comment on what they think the story will be about. Also ask students to predict the plot structure of the story.

READ THE BOOK

SET PURPOSE Have students set a purpose for reading. Their interest in finding out more about Grandma Betty and the girl on the front cover or in Grandma Betty's banjo-playing experiences may guide this purpose.

STRATEGY SUPPORT: PRIOR KNOWLEDGE Activating *prior knowledge* aids comprehension before, during, and after reading. Model and review with students the three types of connections they can make for this reader: text-to-self—learning to play an instrument, text-to-world—listening to music, and text-to-text—books about other musicians. Remind students to also look at the illustrations to activate their prior knowledge.

COMPREHENSION QUESTIONS

PAGES 8 What does this sentence mean: "An idea began to grow in Mrs. Tribula's mind"? *(An idea slowly developed in her mind.)*

PAGES 13–17 What was the sequence of events that led to Grandma getting a banjo? *(Possible response: She started by playing the clarinet; she secretly taught herself to play the banjo; she played at a local music contest and amazed her parents; she played for a friend's father who was so impressed that he gave her his banjo.)*

PAGE 18 Why were Mrs. Tribula and Susan disappointed when Grandma Betty did not want to teach Susan to play the guitar? *(Possible response: They missed hearing Grandma Betty play her banjo.)*

PAGE 23 How was Grandma Betty a positive influence over Susan? *(Possible response: She inspired Susan to appreciate music and secondhand things.)*

REVISIT THE BOOK

READER RESPONSE

1. Possible response: First: learned to read music; second: saw the Elvis Presley movie; third: heard her grandmother's story; fourth: learned the guitar chords
2. Responses will vary.
3. Possible response: The word is made up of *second* and *hand. Secondhand* means that the person who now owns the item is the second person to have the item in their hands.
4. Possible response: The story is in chronological order with occasional flashbacks.

EXTEND UNDERSTANDING Have students discuss the theme of the story. Remind them that the theme is the underlying meaning of the story. Tell them that in this story, the theme is implied. Ask students to brainstorm possible themes and write them down. Then discuss each suggestion one at a time. Ask students to evaluate each possible theme and look for places in the story that support it. Wrap up the discussion when the class has derived a theme that is well supported by events in the story.

RESPONSE OPTIONS

WRITING Have students parody a familiar song and write one original lyric and an original chorus. Assist students as they try to find the rhythm and/or rhyming patterns of the familiar song. Provide time for students to share their parodies with the class.

ELL Encourage students to share music and musical instruments of their native culture. Elicit class discussion of the importance of music in all cultures. If resources allow, offer to play a recording of music from the students' native country.

SOCIAL STUDIES CONNECTION

Time For SOCIAL STUDIES

Invite students to record an oral history. Have students interview an elder member of their family or community about the kinds of music that were popular when they were young.

Skill Work

TEACH/REVIEW VOCABULARY

Have students find the meaning of vocabulary words by using context clues. Ask them to begin with the word *fidgety* in the last paragraph of page 10. Ask students to say its meaning in their own words, then explain which context clues helped them understand the word. Repeat for each vocabulary word.

TARGET SKILL AND STRATEGY

SEQUENCE Describe a *flashback* as a situation where a character in story remembers an event in his or her past. Flashbacks occur on pages 5, 6, and 13. Lead students to recognize that the chronological *sequence* of events in the story is interrupted at times by Grandma Betty recalling events when she was younger. As students read, have them plot a time line to help them understand the order of events of Susan's and Grandma Betty's lives.

PRIOR KNOWLEDGE Remind students that when reading fiction, they can often draw on *prior knowledge* from a similar story they have read or their personal experiences. Have students think about an elder person in their life. Ask them if they share any interests or hobbies with this person, or whether this person influences them in some way. As students read, have them think about their relationship with the elder person and notice similarities and differences between their experiences and the experiences of the characters in the story.

ADDITIONAL SKILL INSTRUCTION

COMPARE AND CONTRAST After students read page 5, ask them if they see a comparison made by the author. Lead students to recognize that Mrs. Tribula is comparing Grandma Betty's enthusiasm when she played a banjo to Susan's enthusiasm as she listens to rock and roll. Have them look for similarities and differences between Susan's interest in music to Grandma Betty's interest in music as they read.

Name ______________________________

Sequence

- **Sequence** refers to the order of events in both fiction and nonfiction. Sequence can also refer to the steps in a process.
- **Flashback** is when a character remembers events from the past. Flashbacks can also be in a sequence in the past and interrupt a sequence in the present or recent past.

Directions Reread the following sentences from *Grandma Betty's Banjo.* Then, decide if the sentences are a flashback or if they are about something that happened in the recent past. Explain what clue words helped you decide.

1. It was a rainy Friday afternoon when Susan Tribula fell in love with Elvis Presley.

____

____

2. That night at dinner, Susan enthusiastically recounted everything she could remember about the Elvis movie.

____

____

3. That entire week, at the end of each school day, Susan raced home and immediately did her homework.

____

____

4. Mrs. Tribula remembered being about Susan's age when a neighbor and friend of the family became quite ill.

____

____

5. By the third time they met for a lesson, Mr. Mike announced that he had an idea.

____

____

Name ______________________________

Vocabulary

Directions Synonyms are words that have similar meanings. Draw a line to match the synonyms.

Check the Words You Know

___**bass**
___**fidgety**
___**jammed**
___**secondhand**
___**clarinet**
___**forgetful**
___**nighttime**

1. nighttime	squirmy
2. fidgety	night
3. forgetful	used
4. secondhand	played music
5. jammed	absentminded

Directions Write a sentence using each of the words below.

6. clarinet ______________________________

____

7. bass ______________________________

____

8. fidgety ______________________________

____

9. jammed ______________________________

____

10. nighttime ______________________________

____

Story Prediction from Previewing

Title ______________________________

Read the title and look at the pictures in the story.
What do you think a problem in the story might be?

I think a problem might be ______________________________

____

____

After reading ______________________________,
draw a picture of one of the problems in the story.

Story Prediction from Vocabulary

Title ______________________________

Look at the title above and the list of words and phrases below.
Write sentences that predict who and what this story might be about.

Words and Phrases

Characters: ______________________________

____

Problem: ______________________________

____

____

____

Events: ______________________________

____

____

____

Outcome: ______________________________

____

____

____

KWL Chart

Topic ____________________

What We Know	What We Want to Know	What We Learned

Vocabulary Frame

Word

Association or Symbol

Predicted definition:

One good sentence:

Verified definition:

Another good sentence:

Story Sequence A

Title ______________________________

Beginning

Middle

End

Story Sequence B

Title ______________________________

Characters

Setting

Problem

Events

____
____
____
____
____
____
____
____
____

Solution

Story Elements

Title ____________________

This story is about ____________________

____
(name the characters)

This story takes place ____________________

____
(where and when)

The action begins when ____________________

____

____

Then, ____________________

____

____

Next, ____________________

____

____

After that, ____________________

____

____

The story ends when ____________________

____

____

Theme: ____________________

____

Question the Author

Title ____

Author ___________________________________ Page _____

1. What does the author tell you?	
2. Why do you think the author tells you that?	
3. Does the author say it clearly?	
4. What would make it clearer?	
5. How would you say it instead?	

Plot Structure

Title ______________________________

Characters ______________________________

Setting ______________________________

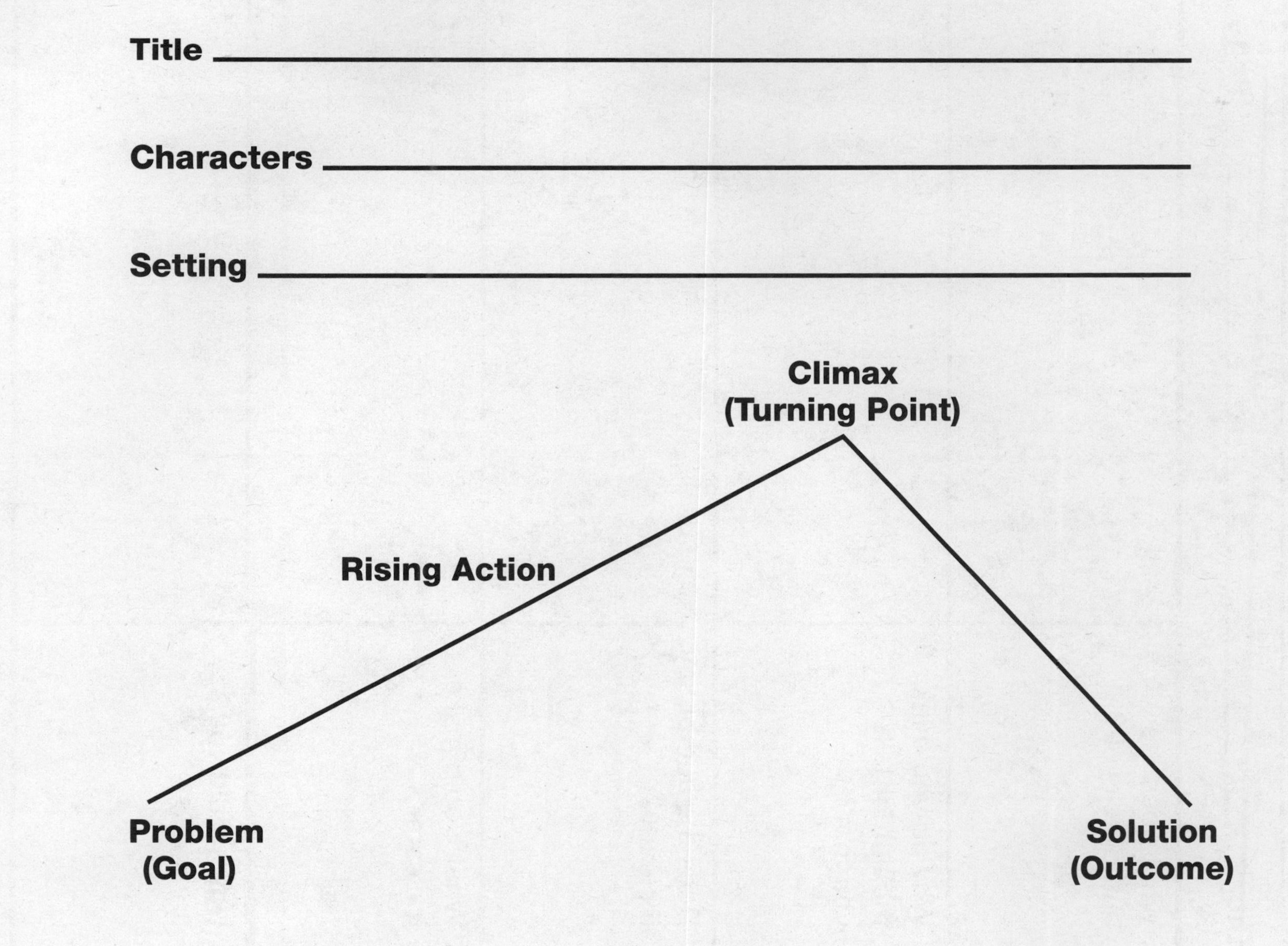

Story Comparison

Title A ____________________

Characters

Setting

Events

Ending

Title B ____________________

Characters

Setting

Events

Ending

Web

Main Idea

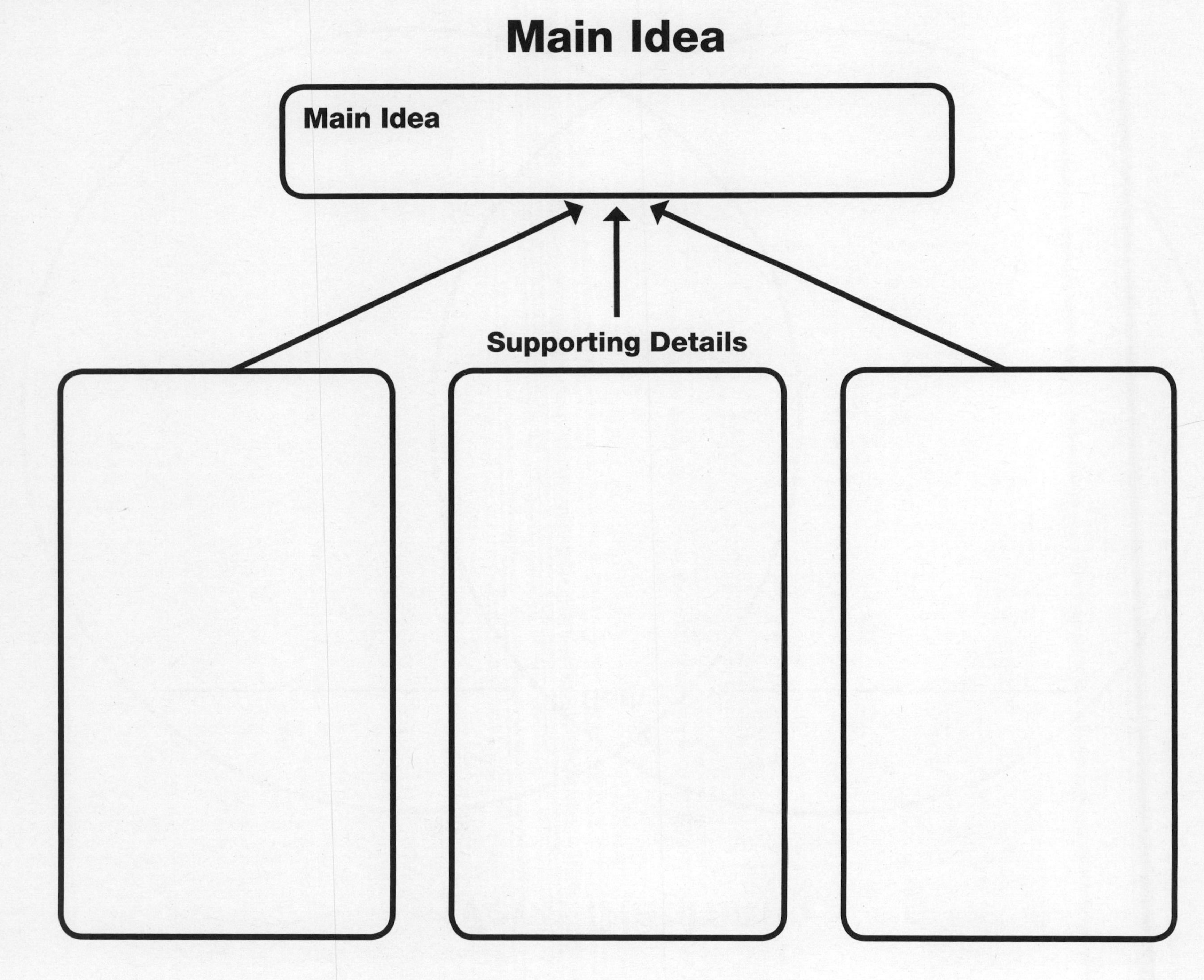

Venn Diagram

Both

Compare and Contrast

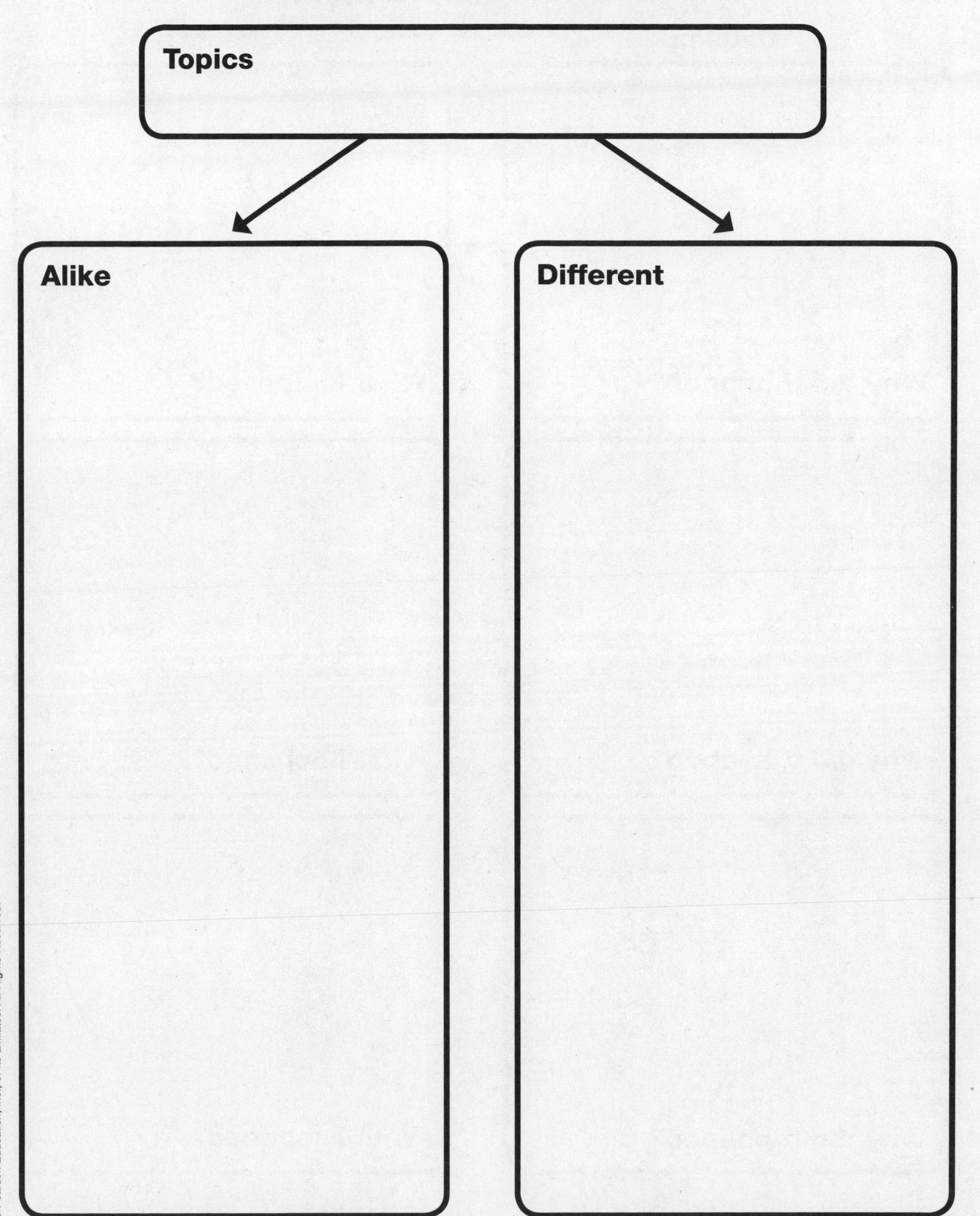

Cause and Effect

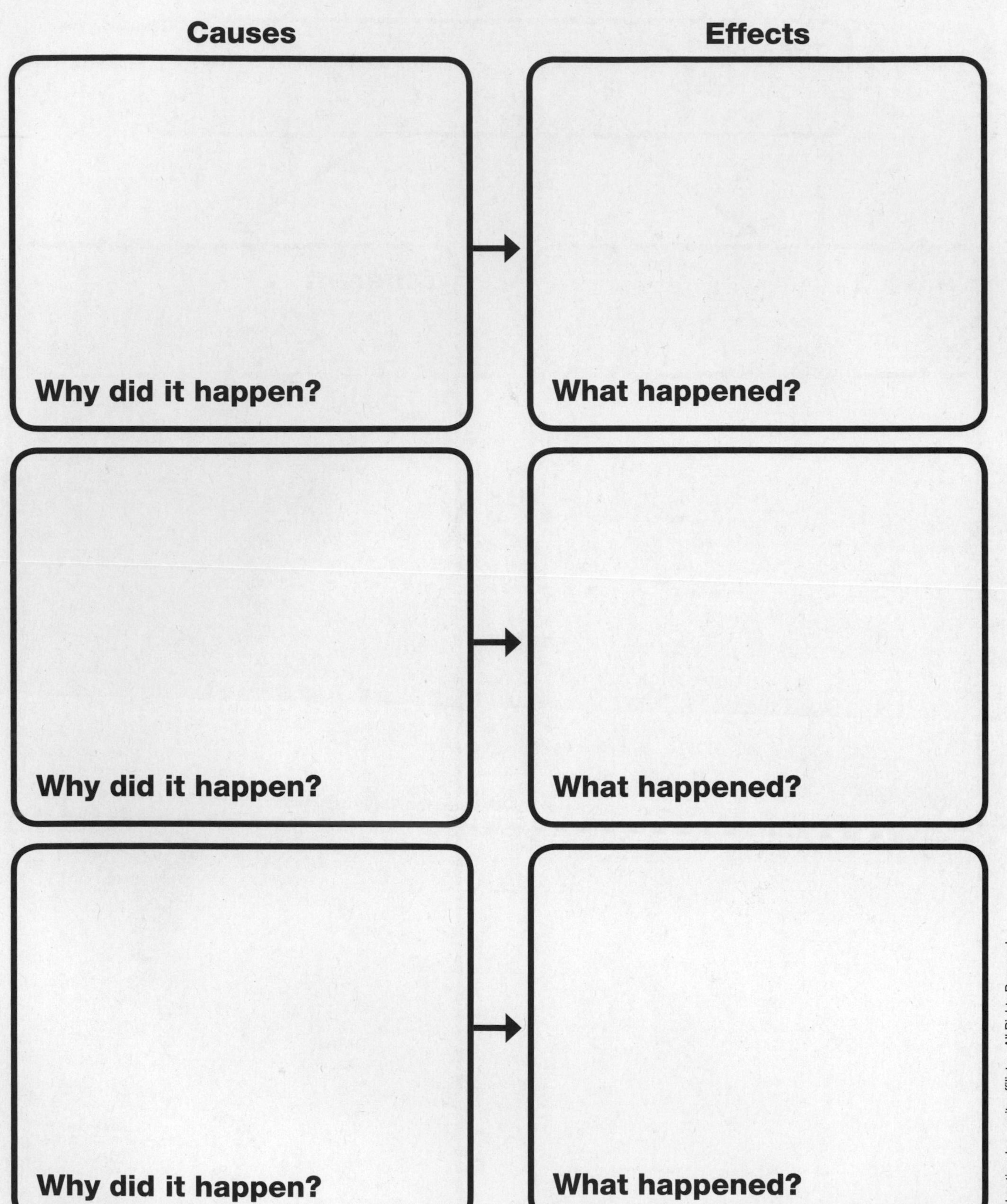

Problem and Solution

Problem

Attempts to Solve the Problem

Solution

Time Line

Date _______ _______ _______ _______ _______

Steps in a Process

Process ______________________________

Step 1

↓

Step 2

↓

Step 3

↓

Step 4

↓

Step 5

Three-Column Chart

Four-Column Chart

Five-Column Chart

Answer Key

Leveled Reader Practice Pages

The Long Trip Home p. 14

CHARACTER AND PLOT

Title: *The Long Trip Home*
Characters: Jake, Uncle Dave, Jake's parents
Setting: Back road leading to Uncle Dave's house in Maine
Problem: The car crashed into a tree.
Events: While driving home in the rain on a back road. Uncle Dave swerved to avoid hitting a stag. The car hit a tree. Because of the remote location, there was no cell phone service. They decided to walk home in the rain using a flashlight. It was very dark and scary. Jake heard noises. They had to walk through a large puddle of rainwater and mud. Jake wasn't afraid when he saw the stag again.
Solution: By the time they made it to the house, the sky had cleared and Jake's parents were waiting for them.

The Long Trip Home p. 15 Vocabulary

1. grumbled
2. intentionally
3. compressed
4. minute
5. insistently
6. neutral
7. normally

Responses will vary but should show an understanding of the vocabulary words.

Storm Chasing Challenges p. 18

CAUSE AND EFFECT

1. Tornadoes occur when a layer of warm air rises through a layer of cold air, making it rotate.
2. Tornadoes can peel bark off trees and flatten houses.
3. Lightning is a release of electricity in the atmosphere.
4. Tornadoes can flip storm chasers' vehicles. Heavy rain and hail can make it hard to see.
5. Possible responses: Yes, because storms are amazing to look at and you can learn a lot about them. I would like to work in a truck with tracking equipment.

Storm Chasing Challenges p. 19 Vocabulary

1. devastation
2. thieving
3. daintily
4. pitch
5. lullaby
6. resourceful
7. branded
8. veins
9. constructed

10–11. Sentences will vary.

Toby's California Vacation p. 22

SETTING AND THEME

1. Channel Islands
2. If everybody respects nature, plants and animals can be saved from extinction.
3. Possible response: Yes, because the setting is a place where animals live undisturbed.
4. Possible response: The Galapagos Islands, a forest

Toby's California Vacation p. 23 Vocabulary

1. kelp
2. gnawed
3. shellfish
5. sinew
6. headland
7. lair

8–10. Sentences will vary but should show an understanding of the vocabulary words.

Famous Women in Sports p. 26

FACT AND OPINION

Facts: In the 1800s women were allowed to play very few organized sports; One female athlete was Mildred Didrikson; She was given the nickname "Babe"; Babe won two gold medals for track and field in the 1932 Olympics; She would have won a third but was disqualified by the high jump judge; Didrikson died in 1956.
Opinion: By the beginning of the 1900s, change was in the air; People thought Didrikson played baseball as well as Babe Ruth; She is still remembered as one of the greatest athletes ever, male or female.

Famous Women in Sports p. 27 Vocabulary

1. fastball, outfield, windup
   Definitions will vary but should show an understanding of the vocabulary words.
2. doubt
3. ordinary
4. strength
5. the act of laughing at; making fun of

6–8. Sentences will vary but should show an understanding of the vocabulary words.

A Railroad Over the Sierra p. 30

CAUSE AND EFFECT

Possible responses:

1. The transcontinental railroad was built.
2. Cause: The Chinese escaped from China because of political problems, poverty, and overcrowding.
   Effect: San Francisco was heavily populated with Chinese immigrants.
3. The Chinese showed their reliability, strength, and intelligence.

A Railroad Over the Sierra p. 31 Vocabulary

1. prying
2. lurched
3. deafening
4. surveying
5. barren
6. previous

7–9. Sentences will vary but should show an understanding of the vocabulary words.

Sea Life p. 34

COMPARE AND CONTRAST

1. Both are dry for much of the day; sea life is present in both.
2. The high tide zone is wetter than the splash zone.
3. black lichens and varieties of snails
4. They must be able to live out of the water for much of the day.

Sea Life p. 35 Vocabulary

1.	hammock	5.	sternly
2.	concealed	6.	lamented
3.	sea urchins	7.	algae
4.	tweezers	8.	driftwood

Sentences will vary but should show an understanding of the vocabulary words.

A Spy in Disguise p. 38

SEQUENCE

1. Emma Edmonds disguised herself as Frank Thompson and worked as an army nurse.
2. Emma disguised herself as a male African American slave to spy on the Confederate army.
3. Disguised as an Irish woman, Emma cared for a dying Confederate soldier.
4. Disguised as an African-American washerwoman, Emma passed information from a Confederate officer on to Union officers.
5. Charles Mayberry was arrested with southern spies.
6. Emma became ill, and Frank Thompson was listed as a deserter from the army.
7. Emma wrote a book about her adventures.
8. Emma received retirement pay for being a war veteran.

A Spy in Disguise p. 39 Vocabulary

Across		Down	
1.	quarrel	2.	Union
4.	Confederacy	3.	rebellion
6.	stallion	4.	canteen
		5.	glory

7. Sentences will vary but should show an understanding of the vocabulary words.

Abuela's Gift p. 42

COMPARE AND CONTRAST

1. In America, Lupe speaks English. In Mexico, she speaks Spanish.
2. Lupe's friends at home don't celebrate the Three Kings.
3. It is Lupe's grandmother, not Lupe's mother, who teaches Lupe to make the pastry.
4. smell of hot chocolate, smell of the wood stove, lots of cooking, family together
5. Possible response: Using the skill of comparing and contrasting helped me better understand the differences of how Mexican families celebrate Christmas.

Abuela's Gift p. 43 Vocabulary

Underline sentences 2, 5, 6, and 8.

10–12. Responses will vary but should use the vocabulary words correctly within the sentences.

Helping Others p. 46

AUTHOR'S PURPOSE

Possible responses:

1. The author's main purpose is to inform readers about different ways that people have tried to help others.
2. The writer probably included this section to persuade readers to find a way to help others.
3. It supports the purpose of persuading readers to find a way to help others.
4. Possible response: to show that even children can help others in need.

Helping Others p. 47 Vocabulary

1.	jostled	5.	turquoise
2.	bracelet	6.	mesa
3.	Navajo	7.	bandana
4.	hogan		

Paul Revere and the American Revolutionary War p. 50

AUTHOR'S PURPOSE

Possible responses:

1. to inform; I think the author wanted to give readers more information about Paul Revere and the events leading up to the American Revolution.
2. So you the reader can compare and contrast the two styles of dress and weaponry.
3. The author uses headings to organize the information into sections.; Responses will vary, but students should include two interesting facts about a heading from the story.
4. I think she ended the story this way to reflect the uncertainty people had about what would happen next. This story is not about the actual war, but the events that lead to it.

Paul Revere and the American Revolutionary War p. 51 Vocabulary

1.	uncontrolled event	5.	increased
2.	unafraid	6.	solemn
3.	faint light	7.	horse
4.	stays		

Possible response: Maybe it was *fate* that led the colonists and the British to fight against one another. Their early battles over taxation ended up being *magnified* to the point where one *fearless* soldier was pitted against the other—the British on his *steed*, and the *colonist* often on foot. The colonists took the *somber* news of taxation badly, because they did not even have the *glimmer* of a voice in the British government. The memory of their hard–won battle *lingers*, as we remember their contribution.

The Search for a Perpetual Motion Machine p. 54

SEQUENCE

1. First, a round metal ball rolled up a sloping channel toward a magnet
2. Next, just before it reached the magnet, the ball was supposed to fall through a hole.
3. Then, another channel below, a curved one, would carry the ball back to its start place.
4. Last, it would start up the slope again.

The Search for a Perpetual Motion Machine

p. 55 Vocabulary

1–5. Sentences will vary but should use the vocabulary words correctly.

6. c
7. e
8. a
9. b
10. d

The Italian Renaissance and Its Artists p. 58

MAIN IDEA AND DETAILS

Possible responses:

1. Artists shifted to a style of art called *humanism*.
2. Their paintings focused less on religious teachings.
3. They focused more on human emotions.
4. They focused more on the drama of everyday life.

The Italian Renaissance and Its Artists p. 59

Vocabulary

1. accomplished
2. person who designs buildings
3. alloy of copper and tin
4. big gun
5. gloomy
6. formed
7. the middle of
8. person who tries to understand the nature of reality
9. competitor

10–14. Sentences will vary but should use the vocabulary words correctly.

Searching for Dinosaurs p. 62

FACT AND OPINION

1. opinion
2. opinion
3. fact
4. opinion
5. fact
6. opinion
7. fact
8. opinion

Possible responses for 9–10:

9. Fact: In 1842 Owen first used the word *dinosauria,* from which "dinosaur" comes.
10. Opinion: today the field of dinosaur paleontology is thriving thanks to the efforts of scientists worldwide.

Searching for Dinosaurs p. 63 Vocabulary

1. tidied
2. occasion
3. foundation
4. workshop
5. proportion
6. erected
7. mold

Sentences will vary but should use the vocabulary words correctly.

Blues Legends p. 66

MAIN IDEA AND DETAILS

Main Idea: Ray Charles had a difficult childhood to overcome.

Supporting Details: Grew up during the Depression; family had little money. Began losing his sight at age six. Lost sight by age seven. Father died when Ray was ten. Mother died when Ray was fifteen.

Blues Legends p. 67 Vocabulary

Possible responses:

1. choir: Choir members wear robes.
2. teenager: A teenager may be a puzzle to his or her parents.
3. barber: My barber gave me a haircut.
4. released: Balloons were released at the party.
5. appreciate: We appreciate your kind words.
6. religious: Ministers are religious leaders.
7. slavery: Slavery ended in the United States in 1865.

Computers in Filmmaking: Very Special Effects

p. 70

GRAPHIC SOUCES

Possible responses:

1. a chart
2. Computer-based movies cost less to make and distribute than regular movies.
3. They take up a lot of space as computer files.
4. It would be expensive, so they might have to raise ticket prices.
5. They can see a result immediately.
6. drawback, disadvantage
7. benefit, advantage, strength
8. In favor, because the special effects are really great. Opposed, because ticket prices may go up and because they look grainy on a big screen.

Computers in Filmmaking: Very Special Effects

p. 71 Vocabulary

1. prehistoric
2. background
3. miniature
4. reassembled
5. landscape
6. reassembled
7. landscape
8. background
9. miniature
10. prehistoric

11–12. Sentences will vary but should show an understanding of the vocabulary words.

Journey to the New World p. 74

DRAW CONCLUSIONS

Possible responses:

1. They expected to find the colony guarded by soldiers.
2. English soldiers had been sent to guard the settlement. Roanoke leaders wouldn't allow the island to be totally abandoned.
3. They had trouble growing food and were not able to make friends with the local inhabitants.
4. They ran low on supplies and they encountered difficulties with local Indians.
5. Jane and her family might likely have decided not to go to the New World if they had known that they would find the soldiers vanished and the fort in ruins.

Journey to the New World p. 75 Vocabulary

1. fleeing	6. blunders
2. inspired	7. envy
3. strategy	8. inspired
4. complex	9. strategy
5. civilization	10. rustling

Wilma Rudolph: Running to Win p. 78

GENERALIZE

Possible responses: Facts—born premature and battled numerous illnesses in her early years; at age six, fitted with a metal brace; she worked hard on leg exercises so that at age ten she walked without the brace; she won a place on the U.S. Olympic track team at age sixteen; she set a world record at the 1960 Olympics even though she had a sprained ankle; she received a long list of awards during her lifetime.

Generalization—Despite childhood illnesses, Wilma had determination and she worked hard to succeed as an athlete.

Wilma Rudolph: Running to Win p. 79 Vocabulary

1. wagged its tail
2. ruffles and lace
3. around the room
4. twisted
5. instead of

6–10. Sentences will vary but should show an understanding of the vocabulary words through context clues.

Changing for Survival: Bird Adaptations p. 82

GRAPHIC SOURCES

Responses will vary but should indicate the locations mentioned in the book.

Changing for Survival: Bird Adaptations p. 83 Vocabulary

1. Woodpeckers, mucus	4. Pelican, specialize
2. Ostriches, scarce	5. sterile
3. Penguins, enable	6. critical

The New Kid at School p. 86

GENERALIZE

Possible responses:

1. that they will be mean to him
2. that he will never make new friends
3. He's afraid of getting lost.
4. He's afraid his teacher may be strict.
5. that they will be nice to him
6. that he will easily make new friends
7. That he won't get lost, or if he does, he can ask for directions.
8. That his teacher may be nice.

The New Kid at School p. 87 Vocabulary

1. strict	4. demonstrates
2. episode	5. cavities
3. combination	6. profile

Paragraphs will vary but should show an understanding of the vocabulary words.

Strange Sports with Weird Gear p. 90

DRAW CONCLUSIONS

Possible responses:

1. Yes, because the equipment is heavy and difficult to move.
2. No, because they don't need to wear protective gear.
3. Yes, because they players wear protective head and hand gear.
4. to make their routine more exciting
5. Possible response: rhythmic gymnastics because I like to dance

Strange Sports with Weird Gear p. 91 Vocabulary

1. limelight	6. somersault
2. bluish	7. hesitation
3. gymnastics	8. cartwheels
4. wincing	9. throbbing
5. skidded	

10. Responses will vary but should show an understanding of the vocabulary words.

Bill Lucks Out p. 94

PLOT AND CHARACTER

Possible responses:

Title: Bill Lucks Out

Characters: Bill Harrison, his parents, Rob, Craig, Ms. Cunningham, Susan, Dan Jenkins

Setting: small town in the U. S. in the present

Problem: Bill wants to get into majors in Little League; needs to interview someone for research project on Vietnam

Events: Bill and friends hope to make majors in Little League. In school, they get assigned topic for research paper. Bill has to interview someone about Vietnam War. His parents introduce him to Dan Jenkins. It turns out that Dan knows a lot about Vietnam and baseball.

Solution: Bill gets into majors, and gets an 'A' on his project.

Bill Lucks Out p. 95 Vocabulary

1. b
2. a
3. c
4. f
5. e
6. g
7. d

Paragraphs will vary.

Explore with Science p. 98

GRAPHIC SOURCES

1. It explains why the people are wearing masks. They are wearing oxygen masks to breathe at high altitudes.
2. Makalu; 27,781 ft.
3. Antarctic Peninsula, Transantarctic Mountains, Victoria Land
4. They are wearing scuba gear. It allows them to breathe underwater.

Explore with Science p. 99 Vocabulary

1. b
2. f
3. d
4. a
5. g
6. c
7. e

Paragraphs will vary but should show an understanding of the vocabulary words.

Sailing the Stars p. 102

AUTHOR'S PURPOSE

Possible responses:

1. to inform
2. The author gives facts and details about China's space program.
3. to persuade
4. The author urges students interested in becoming astronauts to try hard.
5. The author might wish to inform the reader so she can better persuade the reader.

Sailing the Stars p. 103 Vocabulary

1. specific
2. gravity
3. monitors
4. focus
5. role
6. accomplishments

Sentences will vary but should show an understanding of the vocabulary words through context clues.

The Journey Through Earth p. 106

CAUSE AND EFFECT

1. Huge rock plates under the continents move slowly.
2. They fall into the volcano.
3. Toby asked the computer to make the craft cooler.
4. She discovered a hidden laboratory full of fossils.
5. A fossil is formed.
6. Toby did not read the message to the others.
7. The craft made the adjustments to get the power it needed.
8. It is difficult for scientists to learn about the Earth's core.

The Journey Through Earth p. 107 Vocabulary

1. extinct
2. hideous
3. serpent
4. encases
5. armor
6. plunged

Paragraphs will vary but should show an understanding of the vocabulary words.

The United States Moves West p. 110

GENERALIZE

1. valid
2. faulty
3. valid
4. faulty
5. valid
6. valid
7. valid
8. faulty
9. faulty

The United States Moves West p. 111 Vocabulary

1. scrawled
2. vacant
3. independence
4. economic
5. overrun

Paragraphs will vary but should show an understanding of the vocabulary words through sentence structures.

Driven to Change p. 114

DRAW CONCLUSIONS

1. Possible responses: people live farther from schools, shopping, and jobs; vehicles are vital; animal and plant habitats are threatened or destroyed; rural way of life is disappearing
2. Possible responses: counting mileage for a prize; Walking School Bus; Bike Train; peaceful protest to stop driving to school
3. Possible responses: more energy; more endurance; faster metabolism; happier outlook; improved focus; better sleep; stronger body and heart; reduced stress and anxiety
4. Possible responses: less consumption of fossil fuels; less CO_2 released in the air; reduce effects of Global Warming

Driven to Change p. 115 Vocabulary

1. headline
2. roost
3. bizarre
4. high-pitched
5. vital
6. breathtaking

Paragraphs will vary but should show an understanding of the vocabulary words.

The Kudzu Invasion p. 118

MAIN IDEA AND DETAILS

Main Idea: Bringing plants from one country to another is not always a good thing.
Supporting Details: crowds local plant life; no insects to kill it; can grow a foot a day
Main Idea: Kudzu also attacks human-made structures.
Supporting Details: vines pulled down farmhouses; farmers try to protect their barns; destroys power lines

The Kudzu Invasion p. 119 Vocabulary

1. bleached
2. suspicions
3. decay
4. carcasses
5. starvation
6. parasites
7. decay
8. scrawny
9. tundra
10. suspicions

Sentences will vary but should show an understanding of vocabulary words.

The Golden Journey p. 122

COMPARE AND CONTRAST

Possible responses:

River Crossing: Men lead the way. Husband comforts sad wife.

Both: People work together. Valuable item is lost.

Cold Weather: Mother suggests her favorite chair should be used for firewood. Mother is determined.

The Golden Journey p. 123 Vocabulary

1. spoonful
2. precious
3. realm
4. cleanse
5. adorn
6. lifeless
7. c
8. c
9. b
10. a

Paragraphs will vary but should show an understanding of the vocabulary words.

Stop That Train! p. 126

FACT AND OPINION

1. statement of opinion; This is the author's idea about trains. I cannot prove it is true or false.
2. statement of opinion and fact; This is the author's belief. Fact is Casey did die in a train wreck.
3. statement of fact; I can prove this statement is true or false by checking the Internet or in an encyclopedia.
4. *Stop That Train!* is twenty pages long. *Stop That Train!* tells about train accidents of the 1800s.
5. Possible response: In my opinion, this book was very interesting. This book should be read by anyone interested in the history of trains.

Stop That Train! p. 127 Vocabulary

1. cruised
2. drenching
3. hydrogen
4. era
5. explosion
6. criticizing

Possible responses:

Critic: A person who forms or expresses judgment against people or things.

Criticize: to find fault; judge disapprovingly

Criticism: the act of making judgments

Critique: a critical analysis of a subject, like a literary work

Critical: finding fault

Grandma Betty's Banjo p. 130

SEQUENCE

1. recent past—The sentence is about Susan who is the main character in the story. Clue words include *a rainy Friday afternoon*.
2. recent past—The sentence is about Susan. Clue words include *that night*.
3. recent past—Clue words include *that week*.
4. flashback—Clue words include *remembered being about Susan's age*.
5. recent past—Clue words include *third time*. The sentence is about Susan.

Grandma Betty's Banjo p. 131 Vocabulary

1. night
2. squirmy
3. absentminded
4. used
5. played music

Possible responses:

6. Grandma Betty used to play the clarinet.
7. Susan played the guitar while Mike played the bass.
8. Susan had a lot of energy and was very fidgety.
9. Grandma Betty jammed with her friends at the end of the story.
10. Susan would practice the guitar even at nighttime.